Assisting Handicapped Children:

A Handbook for Parents and Involved Professionals

Assisting Handicapped Children:

A Handbook for Parents and Involved Professionals

Earl S. Zehr

Rowan Mountain Press
Blacksburg, Virginia

Assisting Handicapped Children: A Handbook for Parents and Involved Professionals
© Copyright 1992 by Earl S. Zehr
Typesetting by Faulkner Printing, Blacksburg, Virginia.
Printed and bound in the United States of America by
  Professional Press, Chapel Hill, North Carolina.

First Edition, 1992

Library of Congress Cataloging-in-Publication Data

Zehr, Earl S. (Earl Silas), 1933–
    Assisting handicapped children: a handbook for parents and
involved professionals / Earl S. Zehr. — 1st ed.
        p.   cm.
    ISBN 0-926487-11-6
    1. Handicapped children — Care — Handbooks, manuals, etc.
2. Developmentally handicapped children — Care — Handbooks,
manuals, etc.   I. Title.
  HV888.Z44   1992
  649'.151 — dc20   92-26636
                                                       CIP

Rowan Mountain Press, P.O. Box 10111, Blacksburg, Virginia 24062-0111   •   (703) 961-3315

To all the handicapped
people who have
touched my life

CONTENTS

Thinking Activity
Regulation Process – Concept Formation, Memory · Complex
Skills – Problem Solving, Decision Making, Creative Thinking

Specific Learning Disabilities
Reading (Dyslexia), Spelling

Specific Professional Personnel/Agency Involvement

Chapter 4   Physical Body Structural Systems

Manifestation #3 – Expressive Processing

Communication Systems
Speech · Voice (pitch, intensity, quality, flexibility) ·
Articulation · Fluency (stuttering, cluttering)

Language Structure (receptive and expressive)
Types (autism, cri-du-chat, Giles de la Tourette)

Specific Learning Disability
Speaking and Writing

Physical Disabilities
Neurological, Congenital, Musculoskeletal (cerebral palsy,
convulsive disorders, spina bifida, STDs, arthritis, MD)

Health Impairments (organs, metabolic, circulatory, misc.)
Heart, Asthma, Galactosemia, PKU, Diabetes, Hemophilia, AIDS,
Cancer, CF

Motor Development
Tactile, Kinesthetic, Interneurosensory, Vestibular

Skills
Balance, Laterality, Position in Space, Ocular, Body Awareness

Physical Fitness
Strength, Endurance, Flexibility, etc.

Specific Learning Disability
Handwriting

Specific Professional Personnel/Agency Involvement

CHAPTER 1

INTRODUCTION

The handicapped person has never had so many opportunities for educational and vocational advancement in any given society as in our United States of America. Public Law 94-142 and Public Law 95-457 have made provisions, when possible, for the handicapped to be educated with those of a similar age and educational level, namely "least restrictive environment." Since 1975 educational systems have been working to accommodate and regulate educational practices so that the specified conditions can be met individually. This has required a great deal of change on the part of each individual school system. Because of the relative newness of this program, administrators, teachers, parents, auxiliary service personnel, and the handicapped individual him/herself have spent many hours of their personal and professional time to make these necessary adjustments by devising the most effective Individual Education Plan (IEP) for the handicapped person involved. Many have had to change educational practices without a firm understanding of the handicap itself and the possible factors regulating those particular characteristics for education planning. This book is a service guide to help understand individuals who have receptive, mental integration, and expressive problems that will hamper normal educational progress. It also deals with those individuals who are so uncomfortable with their immediate environment that learning fails to take place. Emphasis is placed on the language arts skills and how they relate to the individuals who are classified under Public Law 94-142 for special education services.

Hopefully, this book will serve as a quick source of information to enhance a better understanding of a "labeled" individual. Since so many of the handicaps classified as requiring services under the public law are interrelated due to the body parts affected, special consideration has been given to show interrelationships. Stereotyped handicapped labels, such as visually handicapped, physically handicapped, and other health conditions, can soon develop stereotyped educational plans without taking into consideration the actual factors of the individual which can alter a generalization of the particular label.

The philosophy involved in construction of the book content provides an encyclopedia approach. It was written for the reader to gain basic information. It provides a direction or a source for searching out complete and accurate information that is needed to assist a handicapped individual. Special emphasis has been placed on providing sources of professionals who are trained to assess and provide specific information concerning a particular label. Because each handicapped individual is so unique, parents, educators, and involved personnel need to address the individual first and the handicap second. The need to find the professionals who can best assist in understanding the individual's strengths and weaknesses is the key for the school system to best provide those special educational services that the law requires of them. Special education planning is a cooperative agreement among those professionals who can guide the educational program of that individual. When professionals work together, the individual plan for education places the person first. When a diagnosis of a "label" is given this book will give basic information as well as professional and educational direction.

Learning disabilities encompass those individuals who qualify for services under the Education of the Handicapped Act. Special educational materials and procedures must accommodate those disabilities that interfere with the learning process itself. There are four major manifestations that are fundamental to all handicapped individuals who automatically need educational adjustment because of the part of the physical body involved. These four manifestations created the framework for proceeding chapters in this book. They are as follows:

Manifestation 1	Receptive Processing
Manifestation 2	Mental Integration Processing
Manifestation 3	Expressive Processing
Manifestation 4	Emotional Disturbances—involvement in processing

The Education of the Handicapped Act created a special category called Specific Learning Disabilities. Manifestations #1 through #3 have taken those language arts skills that are classified as Specific Learning Disabilities and arranged them separately under the most appropriate manifestation so that interrelationship between academic language arts areas and the Manifestation Learning Disability can be established.

In the book, *Reading, Writing: A Tutorial Guide in the Language Arts*, each language arts skill has been addressed according to an educational continuum. This book provides the needed educational objectives that can provide the basis for an IEP where language arts deficiencies are concerned. The book gives short term objectives and appropriate activities that will enhance all language arts skills. It accommodates the material located in this book.

Each manifestation has the same format. To further enhance the effectiveness of the following chapters, each part of the format design is explained here.

A. Introduction Components

1. **Qualifying definition:** This gives the specific handicap found in the law and its definition.

2. **Vocabulary:** A basic vocabulary is established at the beginning of each specialized disability section in order to give a fundamental knowledge of terms involved or used in that section.

3. **Checklist:** A checklist includes the possible symptoms that might be indicators of this manifestation learning disability. It is designed for characteristics that might be observed that lead to a professional source for assistance.

B. Incidental Involvement

1. **Incidental errors:** Often times observations and judgements are assumed. Incidental errors are possible diagnosis of labels that may be associated with the manifested learning disability but are not necessarily the basic source of the problem and tend to lead into an inappropriate educational direction.

2. **Functional errors:** The basic problems that are involved with a particular learning disability classified in that Manifestation category are addressed. Usually a general description is given so that a basic understanding can be reached. It provides a point of reference for referral to the proper professional source for a more complete under-standing of the disability or the irregular growth of natural development.

C. Fundamental Involvement Possibilities

The Education of the Handicapped Act stipulates that each specified learning disability be explained to the point that learning deficiencies be addressed. Educational services and related services are provided in this section for choices and appropriate actions.

D. Agency Assistance

Names of federal, state, and disability agencies are provided so that a more complete picture evolves. This source is most useful to parents who have little knowledge concerning the general categorical label. Disability agencies are particularly supportive and provide a wide source of information to assist the individual with that disability.

Two continuous sources of general information for this book include:

NICHCY
National Information Center for Children
  and Youth with Handicaps
P.O. Box 1492
Washington, DC 20013

and

HEATH RESOURCE CENTER
American Council on Education
1 DuPont Circle
Washington, DC 20036-1193.

NICHCY provides free fact sheets supplying basic information. Data sheet material on any aspect of Children with Handicaps can be obtained by writing to the above address. Much information was made available to the author for this book from NICHCY. HEATH is the National Clearinghouse on Post-secondary Education for Handicapped Children. The fact sheets and material packets on many types of disabilities are made available free upon request. The *Resource Directory* was especially helpful in writing this book as well as fact sheets obtained through its office.

This book was authored by a parent of an educationally handicapped individual, a special education teacher trainer, and a person who himself has recently received a medical label affecting a key educational skill.

Hopefully, this book unites the prospectives of special education so that the information presented can help facilitate a more systematic understanding of the factors involved so that the handicapped individual him/herself will be better served.

Recently the author observed a bumper sticker that said *Let My Handicapped Go*. It exhibits the indulging philosophy in this book.

Physical Structure for All Individuals
Suffering with Handicapping Characteristics

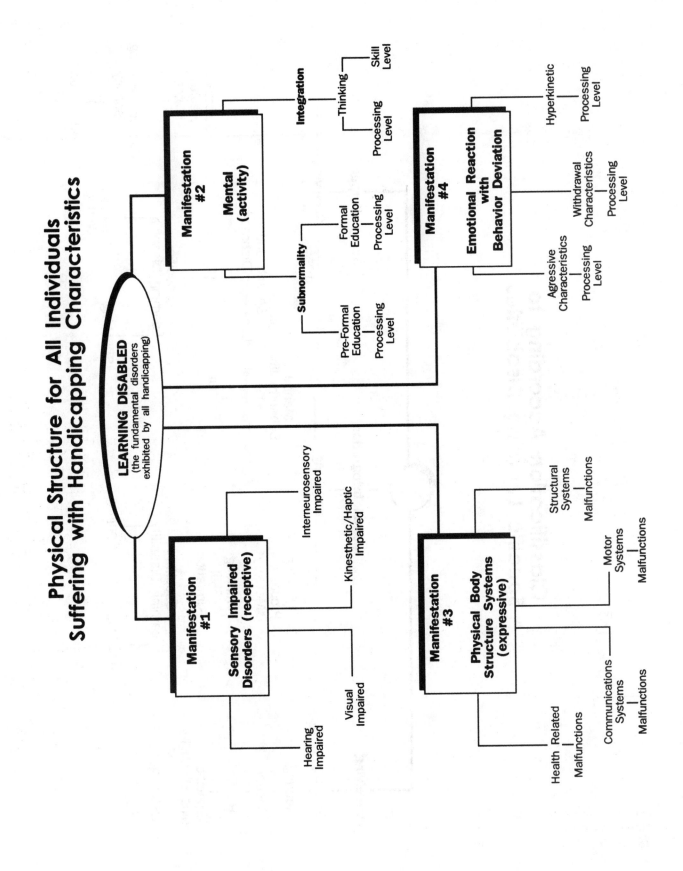

Classification According to Specific Learning Disabilities

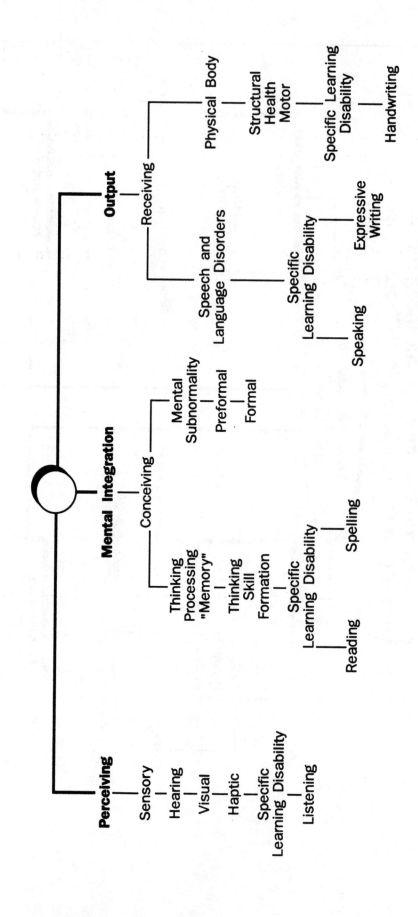

CHAPTER 2

Manifestation #1 – Receptive Processing

SENSORY IMPAIRED SYSTEMS

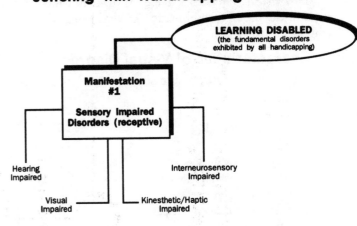

Physical Structure for All Individuals
Suffering with Handicapping Characteristics

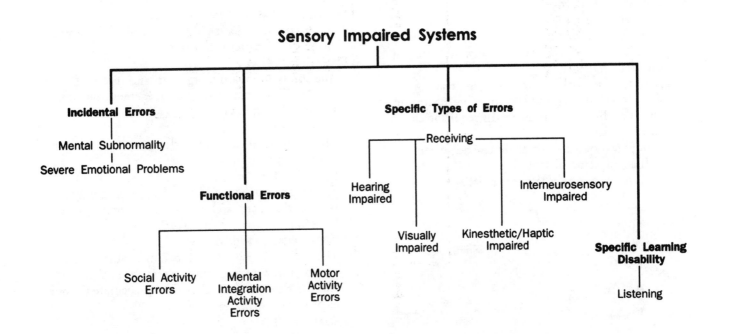

Sensory Impaired Systems

1. Visually Impaired Disorders

Definition by PL 94-142:

"A visual impairment which, even with correction, adversely affects a child's educational performance. The term includes both partially seeing and blind children."

The classification for the "legally blind" requires a visual acuity of 20/200 or less in the better eye. They must rely on touch and hearing.

The classification for the "partially sighted" is that they must have a visual acuity of between 20/70 and 20/200 with corrective lenses. Other qualifying factors include diseases of the eye or other body organs that may slowly or eventually affect vision, and ophthalmologists or educational authorities that deem special consideration is essential for an appropriate education.

"Low vision" refers to a severe impairment which requires the use of a combination of visual and other senses to learn.

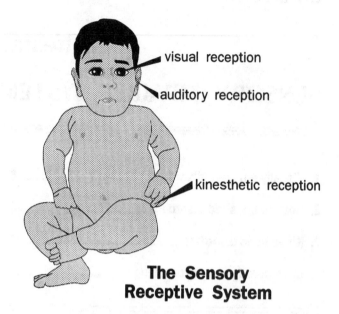

The Sensory Receptive System

Characteristics of Visual Disorders
Observable Signs

Eyes themselves
- Red eyelids
- Crusts on lids/lashes
- Frequent sties/swollen lids
- Reddened or watery eyes
- Crossed or unstraightened eyes
- Pupils of different sizes
- Excessive eye movement patterns
- Drooping eyelids

Visual Behavior Patterns
- Frequently rubs eyes
- Shut/covers one eye
- Tilts head/positions head in a forward direction
- Oversensitive to light
- Avoids close work requiring eye use (reading)
- Facial distortions (blinking, frowning, squinting)
- Irregular distance with materials requiring close work (reading)
- Complains of aches/pains (headaches, dizziness)
- Difficulty seeing distant objects
- Reverses or confuses letters (cande)

SPECIFIC VISUAL SKILLS
Visual Efficiency

Visual efficiency is the ability to perform visual skills in different situations with ease and comfort. These visual skills include eye movements, physical environmental factors, focusing to visual stimuli, and processing information with effectiveness and speed. Visual impairment may result when one of these skills fails. Various terms are assigned to show these characteristics of performance skills. They are as follows:

VISUAL DISCRIMINATION
The ability to visualize likenesses and differences in shape, color, pattern, and size.

VISUAL PERCEPTION
The ability to identify, organize, and interpret stimuli. This involves the physical environmental factors relating to vision.

VISUAL ACUITY
The keenness of the eye's performance as a receptive sensory organ.

VISUAL CLOSURE
The task of perceiving wholes from seeing only parts of that whole, e.g., a clock with no numbers, a word by seeing only part of the word.

FIGURE GROUND PERCEPTION
The ability to select the important components of the environment, e.g., may reverse the background and the figure, fail to select figures accurately, poor at problem solving.

VISUAL IMAGERY
The task of mental reconstruction of sensory experiences.

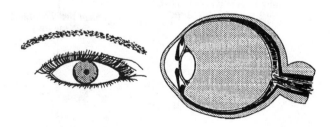

PERCEPTUAL SPAN
The number of words or figures one is capable of perceiving in a single eye fixation.

BINOCULAR VISION
Both eyes acting in unison.

ALTERNATING VISION
Where either eye can maintain fixation and the non-fixating eye is experiencing suppression or inhibition.

VISUAL RECEPTION
The ability to understand and interpret stimuli including symbols, words, or pictures (visual decoding). Visual efficiency may join other receptive processes for the identification, organization, and interpretation of stimuli. Please check the section under interneurosensory functional disorders for additional information.

VISUAL AGNOSIA
The malfunctioning of input sensory channels, although the eye is not impaired, because of impairment of the central nervous system.

SPECIFIC VISUAL SKILLS

Visual Involvement

Incidental Involvement

INCIDENTAL ERRORS

MENTAL SUBNORMALITY
The visually impaired are sometimes labeled as functioning mentally subnormal. They may be so classified because their intellectual functioning is below the average rate. Many experience difficulty in learning because of their visual deficiencies, hence they will score lower when intelligence testing is used as a measurement. Social adjustment also may be difficult when accurate visual functioning is needed. It is important to remember that when the visually handicapped is assessed on traditional intelligence tests, certain illicit responses favor the sighted.

SEVERE EMOTIONAL PROBLEMS
A secondary problem that often appears along with any handicapping conditions is an emotional disturbance. It often occurs because of the frustration of failure to perform normally because of the "main handicap". The typical social behaviors accompanying the visually impaired range from withdrawal (day dreaming) to aggressive behavior (acting out). Hyperactive behavior may become visible. Detailed information accompanying these symptoms is found in the *Seriously Emotionally Disturbed* section of this book.

Functional Involvement

FUNCTIONAL ERRORS

LISTENING SKILLS
The fundamental skill used in the education of all children is listening. The visually handicapped must rely heavily on their hearing sense to obtain their education through public schooling. Modern technology has provided many aids from talking books and tapes to the Kurzwell Reading Machine which converts printed material into spoken English. *Compressed speech* speeds speech electronically which aids the visually impaired. The fundamental skills as developed by the public education system introduce certain skills at certain ages.

SOCIAL SKILLS
"Daily Living"
The visually impaired can adjust to the normal environment with assistance and special training. The daily responsibilities such as grooming, eating, etc., can be taught. Social contacts can be established with the normal population.

ORIENTATION AND MOBILITY SKILLS
Orientation is the awareness of the physical environment that surrounds the individual. Mobility is traveling safely, comfortably, and independently. Instruction for orientation and mobility requires developing motor skills, acquiring basic concepts involved in orientation and mobility, and use of the senses the individual has at their command.

The following skills are suggested as a part of orientation and mobility training:
- Time spent walking from one place to another
- Steps taken
- Curb incidents
- Body contacts made in travel (cane use)
- Total travel time
- Cane instruction
- Methods for crossing streets, etc.

Mobility and orienting materials available include:
- Dog guides
- Canes
- Electronic travel aids (laser beams/high frequency audio waves reflect off nearing object)

Reading-tactile forms:
- Braille—an alphabet based on a system of six dots which requires the use of a stylus and slate that makes indentations in a piece of paper. Tactile orientation is required.

Instructional resource centers provide the blind with the following:
- Braille writers
- Slates and styli
- Cassettes
- Typewriters
- Microcomputers (braille, voice output options)
- Optacon—a device that enables blind students to read regular print; images on the retina of a miniature camera activate tiny pins to vibrate in the shape of the letters so that they can be perceived by fingers.

Reading-auditory forms:
- Readers, talking books as well as Kurzwell Machines and cassettes which allow hearing to prevail as a key to educational learning.

Reading-print forms:
- Includes large type and low-vision aids available through the National Library for the Physically Disabled and Partially Sighted. Any local library can furnish information on attaining such material free.

Writing:
- Includes braille writer, slate and stylus, handwriting, and typewriter.

Computer literacy:
- Microcomputers are available with large print, braille and voice output options. *Only the Best: The Annual Guide to Highest Rated Educational Software* includes information about 185 programs, including source address, grade level, objectives, hardware requirements, cost, and contact information.

> Publisher:
> **R. R. Bowker Company**
> P.O. Box 762
> New York, NY 10011

FUNCTIONAL ERRORS

LISTENING SKILLS
SOCIAL SKILLS

2. Hearing Impaired Disorders

Definition by PL 94-142:
Hearing impairments have been separated under two general classifications for educational consideration. They are as follows:

DEAF
"A hearing impairment which is so severe that a child is impaired in processing linguistic information through hearing, with or without amplification, which adversely affects educational performance."

HARD OF HEARING
"A hearing impairment, whether permanent or fluctuating, which adversely affects a child's educational performance, but which is not included under the definition of *deaf*."

Characteristics of Hearing Impairment

Checklist
Life Orientation

Slight Loss
- Asks for repeated statements
- Understands speech at a distance
- Locates a speech source
- Turns head to the normal ear to listen

Moderate Loss
- Asks for repeated statements
- Turns head to normal ear to listen
- Faces to face conversation good, conversation from a distance poor
- Misinterprets
- Failure to hear high frequency sounds
- Voice quality is flat and lacks inflection in speaking

Marked Loss
- Failure of speech/language development
- Responses to unusually loud sounds
- Amplification produces speech/language

Profound Loss
- Babble and cooing normal but no vocal sounds
- Failure to respond to sounds close by
- Lack of attention after a year
- Laughs/cries but fails to speak
- Failure of amplification for speech/language

Educational Orientation

Behaviors Observed
- General inattentiveness with disruptive behavior
- Attentive to visual stimuli
- Asks repeatedly about directions
- Withdraws socially
- Confused in high background noise levels
- Nods head "yes" even when understanding is lacking
- Allows others to speak for him/her

Medical Conditions Observed
Physical Observations
- Ear discharge
- Cotton frequently observed in ears
- Tired expression early in the day
- Mouth open for breathing

Complaints Given
- Earache
- Complaints of unusual ear noises
- Frequent colds, sore throats, etc.

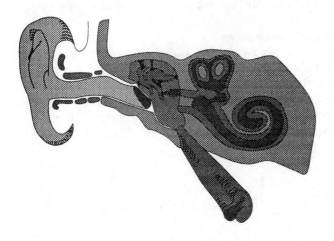

SPECIFIC AUDITORY SKILLS
Auditory Abnormalities

The ear is a very complex organ which offers the opportunity for many physical deficiencies to occur which may affect normal hearing. These abnormalities or dysfunctions include problems with the hearing mechanism itself as well as the sense of hearing. Various terms are used to explain these malfunctions. They are as follows:

AUDITORY AGNOSIA
The malfunctioning of input sensory channels although the ear is not impaired because it is a central nervous system injury.

AUDITORY DISCRIMINATION
The process of an individual's ability to recognize, interpret, and distinguish sound elements and respond appropriately.

AUDITORY PROCESSING
The ability to gather, transmit, decode, and integrate sound signals that originate at the ear and proceed through the central auditory pathways to the temporal lobe in the auditory cortex of the central nervous system. Some useful skills relating to this process include:

AUDITORY MEMORY
The ability to retain and recall information.

AUDITORY SEQUENCING
The ability to recall in a logical order.

AUDITORY BLENDING
The producing of a recognizable word through synthesizing from left-to-right phonemes of a word when pronounced independently.

AUDITORY AWARENESS
The ability to recognize sound changes such as starting and stopping.

AUDITORY CLOSURE
The completion of the spoken word when a certain part of a word or sentence has been started.

AUDITORY FIGURE GROUND
The ability to focus on a particular sound element while non-essential noises are present.

SPECIFIC AUDITORY SKILLS
Auditory Involvement

Incidental Involvement

INCIDENTAL ERRORS

MENTAL SUBNORMALITY
By formal intelligence testing the auditory impaired individual may have lower scores because of the language measurement involved in the test itself. On non-language tests performance is equal to that of the normal child. When intelligence tests are used with the preschool-aged child one should be especially conscious about IQ measurement. Language deficiencies tend to be only identified at this age, with little assistance in language development provided. At three years of age the education system by law is required to provide appropriate instructional help, assist in finding proper amplification devices, and appropriate assessment techniques that favor language improvement.

SEVERE EMOTIONAL PROBLEMS

Although the hearing impaired may have over aggressive or withdrawal types of social behavior often associated with severe emotional problems, they are secondary and the result of being hearing impaired. The key to this problem is lack of communication skills that promote good socialization. Generally, with the hearing impaired, aggressive and/or withdrawal behaviors result because of social isolation encountered when normal communication skills are disrupted.

The social isolation problem may carry over in vocational training where communication becomes so essential. Professional guidance in the psychological/counseling profession needs to be utilized to overcome major communication gaps with peers and coworkers. Personality disorders often occur so services in this area are most helpful.

Functional Involvement

COMMUNICATION SKILLS

There are a variety of communication systems made available in the American culture. The major types used in our society are speaking and writing. For the hearing impaired these selections may become disrupted or even impossible to utilize. Alternate communication systems may be selected and be more acceptable. They include speech, reading, and manual communication (manual signs and fingerspelling). Categorically, when auditory disorders result, alternate methods of communication must be implemented. A selection of combinations are available. They are as follows:

American Sign Language (ASL)

This visual approach presents its own vocabulary, idioms, grammar, and syntax. The individual constitutes handshape, position, movement, and orientation of the hands to the body and to each other. Space, direction, and speed of movement, and facial expression reinforce communication meanings.

Fingerspelling

Fingerspelling is the use of the American Manual Alphabet to spell on your fingers. Often considered "writing in the air," this method is often combined with spoken English and referred to as the Rochester method.

Manual English (PSE)

Pidgin Sign English (PSE) combines English and ASL. Vocabulary of the American Sign Language presented with the fingerspelling results in a 'pidgin' effect.

Oral Communication

This method of instruction combines speech, speech-reading, use of residual hearing, reading, and writing. This method relies heavily on the training of residual hearing. An important factor is beginning the method at an early age (3 years) and providing as much amplification as possible for oral language to take place. Reading, writing, and speech are interrelated to this method.

Speechreading

The speaker's lips, face, and gestures are watched by the hearing impaired to recognize the spoken word. Because 50 percent of the English sounds look like something different and 30 percent of the English sounds are only recognizable by the lip movements, there is a lot of guess work involved, and this method may not be an optimum method for learning oral communication. It can be effective, however, if residual hearing is available for a combined approach.

Cued Speech

This speech-based method is aimed at helping the speech-reading communication method. It uses eight hand shapes in four possible positions to supplement visible lip information.

Simultaneous Speech

Speech, speech signs, and fingerspelling combined to help to speechread what is being spoken and simultaneously read the signs and fingerspelling of the speaker.

Total Communication

Language acquisition and understanding is the goal for the hearing impaired. Acceptance and use of all possible methods to assist in the goal being accomplished is the philosophy of this type of program. This position is becoming increasingly popular in our programs which assist and aid children and adults with auditory problems.

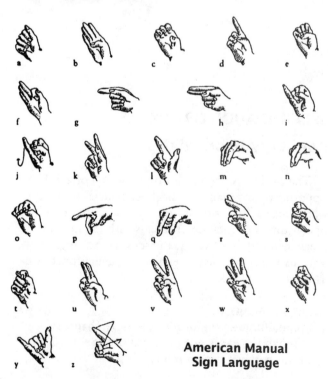

American Manual
Sign Language

FUNCTIONAL ERRORS

SOCIAL SKILLS
"Daily Living"

Adjustment problems relating to social situations and daily living responsibilities stem from the severity in a communication problem of a hearing impaired individual. Social interaction or isolation is dependent on the interaction between a hearing impaired individual and a normal social situation. The responsibility of understanding, interpreting, and responding by verbal language is an extremely complex task. For the hearing impaired this may or may not be possible. It is relatively clear that if it is possible it will be at a much slower rate than normal conservation or an anticipated normal situation. Frustration certainly will become involved.

Natural behavioral responses to such social and/or communication situations may result in the following:

1. A withdrawal from complicated social conversation where more than one other person is involved.
2. A failure of oral responses where background noise accompanies a conservation between the impaired and another person.
3. A desire to develop a social community with fellow hearing impaired individuals excluding normal communication situations.
4. A difficulty in vocational responsibilities where language is extremely essential to performance.
5. A difficulty in marital affairs where communication is a key to successful relationships.

LANGUAGE DEVELOPMENT

The learning process depends largely on mental integration and language. The hearing impaired find the English language difficult to master because of the inability to understand the concept of language and its syntax (example: subject-verb).

As the educational system becomes more complex the following problems develop: (1) sentence structure becomes too complex, (2) sentences begin to exhibit unfamiliar relationships, (3) vocabulary becomes too abstract with unfamiliar concepts, (4) an inability to understand figurative and inferential language.

Academic success is directly related to educational achievement. Because of the complexity of the English language the hearing impaired fall significantly behind. Reading depends upon word meaning comprehension and causes difficulty as well. Emphasis of language development should center around interested vocational avenues which allow a more appropriate and less complicated vocabulary, hence a more meaningful development of the language process.

3. Kinesthetic Disorders

HAPTIC SENSE

A deficiency in the haptic sense is not recognized as a major handicapped disorder under P.L. 94-142. Individuals who have difficulty with touch and motor responses may also exhibit learning disabilities. Academic problems have been traced to receptive sensory processes, particularly in the areas of reading and writing.

Haptic is a Greek based word meaning "moving and doing." The haptic sense is a system by which a person gets information about both the environment and the body. It is the point of environmental contact of the body with the object. It includes the whole body, many of its basic parts, and all of its surfaces. The skin surfaces with the extending appendage of hair growth is a primary sense of touch for temperature, pressure, and pain. Also, the body has the benefit of fingers and toes as attached appendages related to touch. They protrude into the environment permitting an individual to explore through grasping, rubbing, and fingering object qualities such as texture, size, and form. Motor responses are movements in the muscles, tendons, and joints as essential elements involving the haptic sensory process as well.

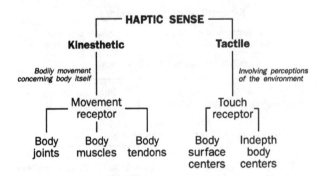

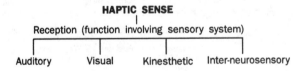

TACTILE SYSTEM

The tactile system is a part of the haptic sensory system involving the sense of touch which includes the surface body centers and the in-depth body centers. Qualities of an object and quantities related to body awareness can be identified and examined through touch. The tactile system is sensitive to temperature regulation.

Specific areas of the body, such as the palms of the hands and the bottoms of the feet, may be over sensitive to the tactile system. Blind and blind-deaf individuals rely heavily on touch for receptive sensory processing.

TACTILE SYSTEM

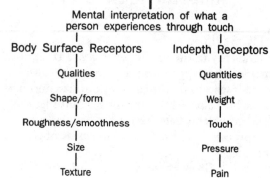

Mental interpretation of what a
person experiences through touch

Body Surface Receptors	Indepth Receptors
Qualities	Quantities
Shape/form	Weight
Roughness/smoothness	Touch
Size	Pressure
Texture	Pain

KINESTHETIC SYSTEM

The kinesthetic sense refers to the information gained by movement. When we purposefully move, a relationship in activity develops. This relationship varies due to resistance to movement or strains in the muscles, tendons, or joints.

Righting reactions, postural reflexes, and balance results in this unconscious set of movement patterns. Knowledge of the body, spatial relationships, and self-image concepts are involved in motor sense.

Kinesthetic Processing

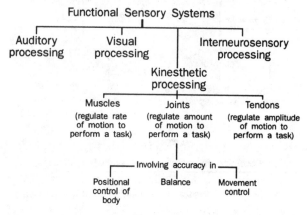

Reception (Information informing the body/body part of its conscious change in environmental position in space)

Functional Sensory Systems

Auditory processing — Visual processing — Interneurosensory processing

Kinesthetic processing

Muscles (regulate rate of motion to perform a task)	Joints (regulate amount of motion to perform a task)	Tendons (regulate amplitude of motion to perform a task)

Involving accuracy in

Positional control of body	Balance	Movement control

Specific Haptic (Kinesthetic/Tactile) Skills

HAPTIC SENSE
The process of getting information through the modalities of movement (Kinesthetic) and touch (Tactile). These sensory stimuli occur from shin receptors for contact, pressure, pain, warmth, and cold.

KINESTHESIS
Sensory stimuli produced by movement or strain in muscles, tendons, or joints.

KINESTHETIC IMAGERY
Muscle imagery cheated by sensations caused by movement of muscles.

KINESTHETIC PERCEPTION
Identification of a message through feeling and touch.

TACTILE
Suggested term for the sense of touch.

TACTILE DISCRIMINATION
The ability to determine sameness or difference between two or more stimuli through the sense of touch/feel alone.

TACTILE PERCEPTION
Interpretation of sensory stimuli through touch.

TACTILE PROCEDURE
Looking and saying a particular word by tracing that word with your finger.

BODY AWARENESS
The conscious recognition and control of the body or a particular body part(s).

SPATIAL RELATIONS
A body awareness of direction, position, and time.

LATERALITY
The awareness of the difference between both sides of the body.

Characteristics of Haptic (Kinesthetic/Tactile)

Any person exhibiting difficulties in touch and motor responses may respond in the following ways:

HOME
- Room is messy, disorganized
- Meals or other organized periods of time are met with interruptions/inability to sit at table.
- Homework time is frequented with other necessary tasks
- Uses gestures when at loss for words
- Always has on the radio, stereo, etc.

SCHOOL
- Uses trial-and-error tasks rather than step-by-step planning
- Doesn't follow through on assignments
- Moves the body or body parts in intense study situations
- Moves frequently during class periods
- Inability to organize materials/assignments
- Fails to follow directions
- Better at being shown how rather than told how

SPECIFIC HAPTIC SKILLS
TACTILE/KINESTHETIC INVOLVEMENT

Incidental Involvement

INCIDENTAL ERRORS

ACADEMIC LEARNING PROBLEMS

Reading and writing academic problems may occur with deficiencies in tactile and/or kinesthetic sensory processing. This is often the case when interneuro-sensory processing (crossmodality) is involved. Visual/haptic and auditory/haptic are two modality functions which fail to function. Visual/haptic deficiencies may appear in poor reproduction of form perception, hence poor reading perception of symbols and members as well.

Poor coordination is the formation of the symbols relating to handwriting skills. The fine differences in letter and word are often not internalized causing these academic learning problems to occur.

Auditory/haptic may also lead to irregularities in speech articulation. This cross-modal problem reflects a deficiency involving motor feeling called rhythm. Unknown words are often attached by putting the pronunciation of the word sounds together (phonics). A lack of speech rhythm may cause difficulty in learning words in such a manner.

Functional Involvement

BODY AWARENESS

Knowledge of the body starts at birth and progresses through adulthood. Body knowledge increases through maturation and development. This includes body planes, body parts, body movements and laterability and directionality.

Large areas of the body are learned first, then discrete aspects of the body are considered. How the body is pictured, attitude toward their body, and capabilities and limitations to the body are included. When knowledge of the body and its environmental surroundings are acquired the child will perform academic learning better.

Body image is a system of ideas and feelings that person has about his/her structure. Perceptions, attitudes, and values gathered from the environment influence this image. Accurate body knowledge results when the environment is meaningful and fulfilling. Self-concept is an important part of the haptic sensory input system.

Observable characteristics include a person's inability to have appropriate posture while sitting, standing, or walking. There is a tendency to bump into objects. A lack of smooth movement and/or timing (clumsiness) may be observed. Lack of knowledge about where certain body parts are located or specific knowledge about that body part's functioning may be lacking. Movement problems may include over/under reaching, difficulty with imitative movement, and inaccurate estimation of body size in relation to people and objects.

FUNCTIONAL ERRORS

SPATIAL RELATIONSHIPS/LATERALITY

The perception of the objects in the environment and how they position themselves to the body may pose a sensory input learning problem. The human body is a reference point for identifying the position of objects in space. Near space surrounds the immediate environment of the person, middle space extends to about 20 feet surrounding the human body, and far space goes to infinity. Judgement in distances, size, and relative positions of objects become involved.

Problems created for failure to perceive proper positioning may include trouble with "up"/"down," "front"/"back," and "left"/"right." Movement under or around objects may cause difficulty. The inability to maintain an appropriate body position around movement of objects may be observed. Sequential tasks or problem-solving situations are found difficult. Spelling errors may be frequent because of these sequential type problems.

LATERALITY

The awareness of differences between the two sides of the body may cause lateral sensory input problems. Balance problems on one or either side may result. The development of the awareness of the two distinct sides of the body comes from an intact vestibular system and kinesthetic sensory system.

Defective characteristics that are observed include avoiding the use of one side of the body, using one limb more often than the other, lack of hand preference in school, work, and daily activities. A great deal of research is being considered on how important dominance is in relation to thinking and learning.

4. INTERNEUROSENSORY PROCESSING

Interneurosensory processing is not recognized as a major handicapping disorder under the laws that mandate special education instruction modification or services. Motor ability and perceptual-motor development occur normally during the first five years of life. Should any one system fail to develop properly, all motor development becomes delayed.

Interneurosensory processing involves the combination of any sensory system with another appropriate for sending sensations to the brain for use. Deficiencies often occur when one system is failing to function or when two basic motor sensory receptive processes are not functioning together properly.

There are various combinations of the visual, auditory, vestibular, kinesthetic, and tactile (basic motor functions) receptive sensory motor skills that perform pertinent tasks in the organizational process. Interneurosensory combinations are identified and defined under each basic motor function.

Specific Interneurosensory Skills

AUDITORY-VOCAL ASSOCIATION
The capacity to respond vocally to auditory stimuli.

VISUAL-MOTOR COORDINATION
The interrelationship of movement and vision.

VISUAL-MOTOR FINE MUSCLE COORDINATION
The coordination of fine muscles included in use of the eye and hand.

VISUAL-MOTOR MEMORY
The visual images reproduced in motor form.

VISUAL-MOTOR INTEGRATION
In complex situations, the ability to effectively accomplish effective interaction of visual-motor skills.

VISUAL-MOTOR SPATIAL-FORM MANIPULATION
The ability to manipulate three-dimensional objects through spacial movement.

TACTILE-KINESTHETIC
The combination of touch and movement for producing sensory impressions.

VISUAL-MEMORY
The capacity to recall visual images after a lapse of time.

AUDITORY-MEMORY
The capacity to retain and recall auditory information.

SPECIFIC LEARNING DISABILITY

SPECIFIC LEARNING DISABILITY
A disorder in one or more of the basic psychological processes involved in understanding or in using language, spoken or written, which may manifest itself in an imperfect ability to listen, think, speak, read, write, spell, or to do mathematical calculations. The term includes such conditions as perceptual handicaps, brain injuries, minimal brain dysfunction, dyslexia, and developmental aphasia. The term does not include children who have learning problems which are primarily the result of visual, hearing, or motor handicaps, of mental retardation, of emotional disturbance, or of environmental, cultural, or economic disadvantage.
(As defined in the regulations for P.L. 94-142)

Specific Listening Difficulties

Receptive/Mental Integration Processing

Listening is fundamental to all communication skills, both verbal and non-verbal. It is the first communication skill used by a baby and the primary skill for success in educational activity involvement. The physical basis of listening is found in the receptive processing involved with the ear and hearing. The brain is involved with processing the listening stimuli by attending/comprehending and assigning pertinent meaning. Hence, listening is complex and its educational involvement is crucial. Failure to develop listening skills affects speaking, reading, and writing as well.

Vocabulary

EAR
The basic physical source of listening

COMPREHENSION
The understanding and interpretation of an image, idea, or feeling.

ATTENTION
The maintaining of focus on communication skills being transmitted.

EVALUATION
A term frequently used to denote the importance of critical mental processing of the image, idea, or feeling.

RECEIVING
The physical processing of sound accepted by the brain for mental processing.

CRITICAL LISTENING
The ability to detect propaganda devices used to persuade/interpret the communicator.

LISTENING ENJOYMENT
Pastime involvement activity in the aesthetic (music, drama, discussion); for entertainment/appreciation.

EMOTIONAL LISTENING
The interpretation of both verbal and non-verbal responses of an individual for the purpose of understanding feelings.

AUDITORY DISCRIMINATION
The physical basis of hearing involving sound likenesses and differences.

AUDITORY RECEPTION
The brain's inability to understand what is heard.

Checklist

· Hears vowels, consonants, and syllables accurately
· Recognizes a particular sound in various positions of the word
· Discriminates between sound (high/low, soft/ loud)
· Discriminates various sound sources accurately
· Follows a rhythm pattern
· Imitates a sequence pattern after hearing it
· Relates feelings about an incident or event
· Relates feelings about a song, poem or story
· Follows a series of directions
· Relates a message
· Contributes to a group discussion
· Relates information from an oral presentation, TV program, etc.
· Recalls accurately
· Carries on an intelligent conversation
· Uses the telephone effectively
· Relates a story from a favorite TV program
· Selects a main idea from a story or program
· Draws conclusions of a logical nature
· Distinguishes between truth and fantasy
· Identifies synonyms and antonyms accurately
· Sequences stories with accuracy

INCIDENTAL ERRORS

HEARING IMPAIRED

Physiological basis for a listening disability may result from faulty auditory processing. Failure to hear, distinguish sound differences and recognize word patterns will indicate conductive and neurosensory hearing losses. Since the source of listening is based primarily on hearing, serious educational involvement may be encountered.

SERIOUSLY EMOTIONALLY DISTURBED

Emotional imbalances may lead to a child's inability to master listening readiness and the basic skill itself. Tension and poor social adjustment may compete with the attending processes of listening (failure to focus on a particular communicating stimulus). Readiness in listening skills may be influenced by lack of good experiences in home and cultural environments. Nervousness, boredom, and lack of interest may be descriptive behaviors characterizing an emotional maladjustment.

MENTAL SUBNORMALITY

Subnormal intellectual functioning includes the inability to get meaning from verbal stimuli and the lack of an appropriate vocabulary to gain the word meaning itself. Listening processes affected include comprehension and assigning/evaluating meaning from verbal stimuli and the lack of an appropriate vocabulary to gain the word meaning itself. Listening processes affected include comprehension and assigning/evaluating meaning. Intellectual functioning levels directly influence how effective the listening process can develop with serious educational involvement resulting.

FUNCTIONAL ERRORS

The function of listening involves the striving to understand and be understood. The ability to perform the receptive/mental integration process of listening involves three basic components. Attentiveness development involves the ability to focus on the communication message which includes the reception of the image into the brain for internalization. The brain internalizes the communicated message by selecting and organizing for communication an image so that understanding takes place. Evaluation of the message itself through the skill of thinking creates the preferred desired concept for use.

Functional problems arising from this process include:

· **Lack of interest:** Attentive focusing needs much practice with many happy experiences resulting. For attentiveness to occur, listening activities must be age-appropriate and of interest so that the ability of effective listening will develop functionally.

· **Lack of purpose:** The focus of listening attentiveness needs purpose or the habit of partial listening will result. Listening has two major considerations. One is for information and the other is for pleasure. Bad habits in attentive listening can develop when failure to train for pleasure listening versus informational listening is not addressed and taught independently. Because each type is different, each is important in the communication process of educational involvement.

· **Failure to listen:** The mental processing of thinking skill development is involved. Critical selecting and organizing of the receptive message requires educational instruction. Failure to grasp the necessary organized material through inability to discover the significant points and to evaluate these points interferes with the listening message. The listening process requires an evaluated communication message that functionally engages in worthwhile educational production. This supersedes reading, writing, and speaking in academic area content material.

AGENCIES INFORMATION

International Listening Association
Box 90340
McNeese State University
Lake Charles, LA 70609

R.R. 3 Box 290F
Lake Ariel, PA 18436

RELATED SERVICES

The All Handicapped Children's Act (AHCA) defines related services as "such developmental, corrective, and other supportive services . . . as may be required to assist a handicapped child to benefit from special education." Related services eligibility is based on the law that a child must be "handicapped" and special education is required. A "related service" must be necessary for a child to benefit from special education. A district's responsibility according to the Act was designed to maintain a "basic floor of opportunity." This floor consists of "access to specialized instruction and related services which are individually designed to provide educational benefit to the handicapped child."

Transportation
Transportation is included as a related service under Education of the Handicapped 20 U.S.C. 1404-1461. It is a part of a "free appropriate public education" assurance component stating that transportation must be provided at public expense, under public supervision and direction, and without charge. Its major purpose is to enable a child to be physically present in class.

Transportation must be provided if the district provides transportation for its general school population. Any school district which provides any special education program must provide transportation to any handicapped person qualifying for the particular special education institution or related service. When a

school district does not provide transportation to its general school population it must decide on an individual basis where the transportation benefits the special education of the handicapped individual.

Transportation includes service starting at the vehicle and to the special education and/or related service site or center. It may include to and from residential placement as well. Sites for the visually impaired and hearing impaired where services are found at state facilities, such as the School for the Blind and the School for the Deaf, require of the local school systems a transportation provision. Similar procedures are followed for intersensory handicaps such as the deaf/blind facilities which are geographically difficult to find.

Counseling/Psychological Services
A major component of related services involves both psychological and counseling assistance to handicapped individuals in special education. Public Law 94-142 defines psychological services as including:

"(I) Administering psychological and educational tests and other assessment procedures: (Native tongue required).

(II) Interpreting assessment results:

(III) Obtaining, integrating, and interpreting information about child behavior and conditions relating to learning:

(IV) Consulting with other staff members in planning school programs to meet the special needs of children as indicated by psychological tests, interviews, and behavioral evaluations: and

(V) Planning and managing a program of psychological services, including psychological counseling for children and parents."

Social Work Services in the schools is defined in Public Law 94-142 as including:
"(I) Preparing a social or development history on a handicapped child

(II) Group and individual counseling with the child and family

(III) Working with those problems in a child's living situation (home, school, and community) that affect the child's adjustment in school; and

(IV) Mobilizing school and community resources to enable the child to receive maximum benefit from his or her educational program."

Guidance services are a part of the general education program that participates in the development of an educational plan for each handicapped individual requiring special education related services. The guidance counsellor is frequently the first person to make contact and is in a position to provide continual contact and services. Follow through of individual educational planning and monitoring that progress is often times the responsibility of the counselor.

SOURCES OF PROFESSIONAL HELP

Psychiatrist - A medical doctor specializing in psychiatry or applied behavior disorders.

Psychoanalyst - A medical doctor specializing in a particular field of psychiatry called psychotherapy under the influence of Freud.

Social Worker - Assesses social conditions, interviewing, assists rehabilitation into the community

Neurologist - Focuses on disorders of the nervous system that may influence behavior patterns.

Clinical Psychologist - Performs individual and group therapy sessions, assesses and diagnoses through formal testing procedures—both mental and emotional.

Guidance Counselor - Resides in an educational school site, usually in one building, assisting students who need guidance and counseling in that professional setting.

School Psychologist - Administers and interprets individual psychological and educational tests for gaining information pertinent to an individual educational plan.

Psychometrist - A trained professional in the administration and interpretation of academic achievement and behavioral tests.

Centers for Counseling/ Psychological Evaluation

Child guidance centers - A specialized center staffed with a cluster of trained professionals whose expertise centers around the needs of children.

Hospital psychiatric unit - Specialized areas in general hospital setting designated for intense psychological and counseling services.

Local mental health center - Public facility serving a certain community or designated area and providing services in counseling and psychological assistance. (Cost of services is pro-rated to the economy).

Play therapy - Used with children below the ages of eight, allowing through play to demonstrate how they feel about themselves and who is important in their lives at any designated center.

Group therapy - Interaction within a selected group of individuals to open up and expand communication; used in a designated counseling/psychological center.

Private hospitals - A private setting often centered around a particular philosophy used in treating individuals needing special care.

Psychotherapy - A process or treatment covering various kinds of counseling and guidance, individual, group, child, and family therapy and psychoanalysis.

Psychology - An educational approach studying human behavior using psychological and counseling techniques and procedures.

Medical/Health Services

Medical and health services are for diagnosis and evaluation purposes which help decide whether movement from regular educational programming to special education is essential. Before a child can enter special education a free physical examination from a medical doctor is required. Regulations require "related services" provisions including "school health services." School health services are provided by a qualified school nurse or other designated, qualified person. The service described in the law and its regulations must be reasonable to provide and pertinent to the educational process.

Health information compiled for each child referred to the ARC (Admissions and Release Committee) should contain a written description of medical, physical or pharmacological information which may affect educational performance. The following information may be found in such a report: motor functioning; medication used or on currently; a history of illness and accidents; need for medical assistance; medical limitations; chronic illness; history of drug and alcohol abuse; results of vision and hearing screening; trauma; emotional problems; and previous medical evaluations; services; and hospitalization.

MEDICAL/HEALTH PERSONNEL

School Nurse

The Rules of Special Education 12.17 (1) require a health history as part of the comprehensive evaluation. Professional judgement regarding expanded health evaluations or reports related to potential or identified health problems is a major responsibility. When no health problem is present, a written report is filed into the child's folder. Attendance at individual educational program meetings is expected or information from such meetings should be given in written form to the school nurse. These are the major responsibilities of the school nurse as they relate to special education. The school nurse should assist the handicapped child by providing health care; assist the parents of handicapped children by acting as a liaison regarding health resource sites such as school, home, community; function as a health consultant and resource for school personnel.

Physical Therapist

The physical therapist organizes, develops, and implements a therapy program to minimize the effect of a physical disability or handicapping condition. The specific responsibilities of the physical therapist include: developing gross motor skill development; develop mobility (walking, crawling, wheelchair use, prosthetic devices); recommend equipment and training in the use of adaptive equipment (special chairs, leg braces, positioning equipment); consulting with and training staff in handling/positioning/safety of movements; development and monitoring respiratory functioning programs.

Occupational Therapist

The occupational therapist's role is to minimize the effect of a physical disability or handicapping condition by organizing, developing, and implementing a therapy program of an individual nature. The major roles and responsibilities of the occupational therapist include: a development of fine motor coordination; recommending equipment/training for a student to use in the classroom, for the individual himself, or his/her hand skills (dressing aids, eating aids, special chairs, prosthetic devices, splints); development of sensorimotor skills/sensory integration to classroom performances (motor planning, bilateral integration, tactile defensiveness); develop work simplifications and motor techniques for practical school usage.

School health services are varied from state to state and school district to school district. Many school districts provide little or no assistance in this area because of financial reasons. Health services remain a vital contributor to the special education program in the area of medical and physical facets of the total school program.

SENSORY IMPAIRED DISORDERS

Sensory impaired disorders are directly identified for review and evaluation as a related service. Vision and sensory learning deficiencies are required before an individual is placed in any special education setting. This is at no cost to the individual being evaluated for special education services.

Vision

A screening or comprehensive vision evaluation must be completed before evaluation in education, mental processing (cognitive testing), social competence and vocational can be introduced. When vision impairments are found, referral is made to the appropriate professional.

Ophthalmologist: A physician (M.D.) who specializes in the branch of medicine dealing with the structure, function, and diseases of the eye and their correction.

Optometrist: A nonmedical specialist licensed to work with the measurement of the range and power of vision, examination of the eyes and the prescription of glasses.

Medical Doctor: A physician who works with diseases of the body that influence impairment of vision.

Hearing

Individuals failing to pass auditory preliminary screening must be referred for a free audiological examination. No educational, mental progress testing, social competence, vocational assessments may be given until the completion of the hearing evaluation by an appropriate professional.

Audiologist: A professionally trained person in audiology who is responsible for identification, audiological evaluation, and management of hearing impaired persons.

Otologist: A professional who specializes in the study, diagnosis, and treatment of diseases of the ear and related structures.

Otolaryngologist: A specialist of diseases of the ear and larynx including upper respiratory tract and many diseases of the head and neck.

AGENCY DIRECTORY

Information about a particular handicapping condition is often times not generally available. Parents, educators, health professionals, and everyone else who works with a particular identifiable handicap needs additional information about the handicap, services that are necessary and available, and the location of specified services. National organizations on specific disabilities or conditions focuses on information and support. Parent training and parent support groups offer general information, assistance, and support. Government agencies give information relating to laws and services. When help is needed there are many sources available to the handicapped person. When educational practices and general information appear sketchy and vague, help may be found through knowledgeable centers. These centers may be able to clarify the opportunities available to the handicapped person and a clearer route for the person directly involved with that individual who is handicapped.

Agency listings are given with addresses and telephone numbers when possible. Telephone numbers can, however, be obtained by dialing information in the city where the location is found. Do not give up if addresses are incorrect. Interagency information is available at any government center or clearing house. They are generally courteous and will assist the person when a need has been voiced to them.

The list of agencies used is largely found in a fact sheet distributed by NICHCY–The National Information Center for Children and Youth with Disabilities, P.O. Box 1492, Washington, D.C. 20013.

GOVERNMENT AGENCIES

Interprofessional Information

**Administration for Children,
    Youth and Families**
P.O. Box 1182
Washington, D.C. 20013
(202) 245-0347

**Administration on Developmental
    Disabilities (DHHS)**
329 D Humphrey Building
200 Independence Ave., S.W.
Washington, D.C. 20201
(202) 245-2890

**Bureau of Maternal and Child Health
    and Resources Development**
Parklawn Building
5600 Fishers Lane
Rockville, MD 20857
(301) 443-2170

**District Internal Revenue
    Service - Tax Information**
(800) 424-1040
(800) 424-FORM

**National Institute of Neurological &
    Communicative Disorders**
NIH, Bldg. 31, Room 8A-06
Bethesda, MD 20892
(301) 496-4000

**National Library Service for the Blind
    and Physically Handicapped**
Library of Congress
1291 Taylor Street, N.W.
Washington, D.C. 20542
(800) 424-8567

**Office of Disease Prevention
    and Health Promotion**
National Health Information Center
P.O. Box 1133, Washington, D.C.
20013-1133, (800) 336-4797

Department of Health and Human Services
(Medicare Information and
    Second Surgical Opinion Program)
Health Care Financing Administration
Baltimore, MD 21235

**National Center for Education
    in Maternal and Child Health**
38th and R Streets, N.W.
Washington, D.C. 20625-8400

**National Information Center for
    Children & Youth with Handicaps (NICHCY)**
P.O. Box 1492
Washington, D.C. 20013
(800) 999-5599
(703) 893-6061
(703) 893-8614 (TDD)

**National Institute of Child
    Health and Human Development**
NIH, 9000 Rockville Pike
Bldg. 31, Room 2A03
Bethesda, MD 20892
(301) 496-3454

**President's Committee on Employment
of People with Disabilities**
1111 20th St., N.W., Suite 636
Washington, D.C. 20036-3470
(202) 653-5044
(202) 653-5050 (TDD)

**Public Information Office
National Library of Medicine**
Bethesda, MD 20894
(301) 496-4000

**Senate Subcommittee on
Disability Policy**
113 Hart Senate Office Bldg.
Washington, D.C. 20510
(202) 224-6265

Social Security Administration Hotline
(800) 234-5SSA
(800) 324-0778 (TDD)
(800) 392-0812 (in Mo./TDD)

**Office of Special Education
and Rehabilitation Services**
Clearinghouse on Disability Information
U.S. Dept. of Education
Room 3132, Switzer Bldg.,
330 C St., S.W.
Washington, D.C. 20202-2524
(202) 732-1723, (202) 732-1245

**Volunteers in Service to America
Foster Grandparent Program**
ACTION
Public Affairs Division
1100 Vermont Ave., N.W.
Washington, D.C. 20525

GENERAL INFORMATION

Public Agencies

STATE EDUCATION DEPARTMENT

The State Department staff can answer questions about special education and related services in your state. Many states have special manuals explaining the steps to take. Check to see if one is available. State Department officials are responsible for special education and related services programs in their state for preschool, elementary, and secondary age children.

STATE VOCATIONAL REHABILITATION AGENCY

The state vocational rehabilitation agency provides medical, therapeutics, counseling, education, training, and other services needed to prepare people with disabilities for work. This state agency will provide you with the address of the nearest rehabilitation office where you can discuss issues of eligibility and services with a counselor. The state vocational rehabilitation agency can also refer you to an independent living program in your state. Independent living programs provide services which enable adults with disabilities to live productively as members of their communities. The services might include, but are not limited to, information and referral, peer counseling, workshops, attendant care, and technical assistance.

OFFICE OF STATE COORDINATOR OF VOCATIONAL EDUCATION FOR HANDICAPPED STUDENTS

States receiving federal funds used for vocational education must assure that funding is used in programs which include students with handicaps. This office can tell you how your state funds are being used and provide you with information on current programs.

STATE MENTAL RETARDATION/DEVELOPMENTAL DISABILITIES AGENCIES

The functions of state mental retardation/developmental disabilities agencies vary from state to state. The general purpose of this office is to plan, administer and develop standards for state/local mental retardation/developmental disabilities programs provided in state-operated facilities and community-based programs. This office provides information about available services to families, consumers, educators and professionals.

STATE DEVELOPMENTAL DISABILITIES COUNCIL

Assisted by the U.S. Department of Health and Human Services' Administration on Developmental Disabilities, state councils plan and advocate for improvement in services for people with developmental disabilities. In addition, funding is made available for time-limited demonstration and stimulatory grant projects.

STATE MENTAL HEALTH AGENCIES

The functions of state mental health agencies vary from state to state. The general purposes of these offices are to plan, administer, and develop standards for state and local mental health programs such as state hospitals and community health centers. They can provide information to the consumer about mental illness and a resource list of contacts where you can go for help.

PROTECTION AND ADVOCACY AGENCY AND CLIENT ASSISTANCE PROGRAM

Protection and advocacy systems are responsible for pursuing legal, administrative and other remedies to protect the rights of people who are developmentally disabled or mentally ill, regardless of their age. Protection and advocacy agencies may provide information about health, residential, and social service in your are. Legal assistance is also available.

The Client Assistance Program provides assistance to individuals seeking and receiving vocational rehabilitation services. These services, provided under the Rehabilitation Act of 1973, include assisting in the pursuit of legal, administrative, and other appropriate remedies to ensure the protection of the rights of individuals with developmental disabilities.

PROGRAMS FOR CHILDREN WITH SPECIAL HEALTH CARE NEEDS

The U.S. Department of Health and Human Services' Office of Maternal and Child Health and Resource Development provides grants to states for direct medical and related services to children with handicapping conditions. Although services will vary from state to state, additional programs may be funded for retraining, research, special projects, genetic disease testing, and counseling services. For additional information about current grants and programs in your state, contact:

National Center for Education in Maternal and Child Health
38th and R Streets, NW
Washington, D.C. 20057.

UNIVERSITY AFFILIATED PROGRAMS

A national network of programs affiliated with universities and teaching hospitals, UAPs provides interdisciplinary training for professionals and paraprofessionals and offers programs and services for children with disabilities and their families. Some UAPs provide direct services for children and families. Individual UAPs have staff with expertise in a variety of areas and can provide information, technical assistance, and inservice training to agencies, service providers, parent groups, and others.

A listing of all University Affiliated Programs may be obtained by contacting:

The Maternal and Child Health Clearing House
38th and R Streets, N.W.
Washington, D.C. 20057.

DISABILITY AGENCIES

Hearing Impairments

Alexander Graham Bell Association for the Deaf
3417 Volta Place, N.W.
Washington, D.C. 20007

National Association of the Deaf (NAD)
814 Thayer Avenue
Silver Spring, MD 20910

National Hearing Aid Society
20361 Middlebelt Rd
Livonia, MI 48152

American Society for Deaf Children (ASDC)
814 Thayer Avenue
Silver Spring, MD 20910

National Information Center on Deafness
Gallaudet University
800 Florida Avenue, N.E.
Washington, D.C. 20002

Visual Impairments

American Council of the Blind
1155 15th St., N.W., Suite 720
Washington, D.C. 20005

National Association for the Visually Handicapped
22 W. 21st Street, 6th floor
New York, NY 10010

American Foundation for the Blind
15 W. 16th Street
New York, NY 10011

Learning Disability Agencies

Association for Children and Adults with Learning Disabilities
4156 Library Road
Pittsburgh, PA 15234

Council for Learning Disabilities
P.O. Box 40303
Overland Park, KS 66204

National Center for Learning Disabled
99 Park Avenue, 6th Floor
New York, New NY 10016

CHAPTER 3

Manifestation #2 – Mental Integration Processing

MENTAL FUNCTIONAL PROCESSING AND DISORDERS

Physical Structure for All Individuals
Suffering with Handicapping Characteristics

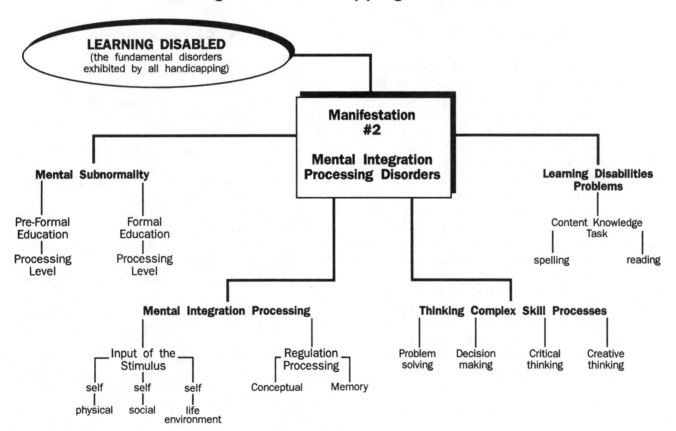

Mental Subnormality

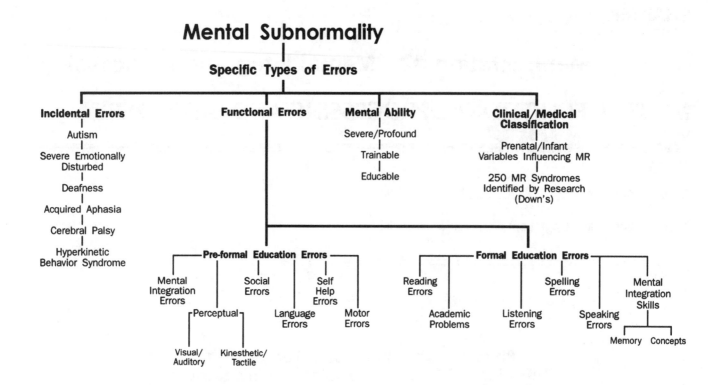

Specific Types of Errors

Incidental Errors
- Autism
- Severe Emotionally Disturbed
- Deafness
- Acquired Aphasia
- Cerebral Palsy
- Hyperkinetic Behavior Syndrome

Functional Errors

Mental Ability
- Severe/Profound
- Trainable
- Educable

Clinical/Medical Classification
- Prenatal/Infant Variables Influencing MR
- 250 MR Syndromes Identified by Research (Down's)

Pre-formal Education Errors
- Mental Integration Errors
- Perceptual
  - Visual/Auditory
  - Kinesthetic/Tactile
- Social Errors
- Language Errors
- Self Help Errors
- Motor Errors

Formal Education Errors
- Reading Errors
- Academic Problems
- Listening Errors
- Spelling Errors
- Speaking Errors
- Mental Integration Skills
  - Memory
  - Concepts

Mental Function Processing

Many learning disabled individuals qualify for special education services because of their failure to respond or perform in academic settings. The mental level or the ability of the brain to function properly may seriously hamper normal intellectual growth. Mental subnormal conditions often classified as mental retardation hamper such progress. The general intellectual functioning level can be measured by assessing the child's ability in relation to what his or her peers can do at a similar age. This is called psychological testing. Similarly, an inability to assess and process incoming stimuli normally can cause affected persons problems in expression of writing, and speaking as well as an inability to read the printed word. This mental integration problem is classified as thinking. Many educators and psychologists classify it under the term cognition. For the purposes of this book we will call it mental integration functioning because our concern is the functioning of the individual to the surrounding environment and the academic functioning disabilities that may deter normal educational progress.

1. MENTAL SUBNORMALITY

Mental subnormality includes those individuals who function below the normal range of mental ability both intellectually and socially. They have difficulties in both learning and social living skills. It is not a disease nor should it be confused with mental illness. Mental retardation extends into adult life where learning continues at a slow and difficult rate.

Mental subnormality may be classified under two major categories. There are those individuals who can reach adulthood with the ability to perform the basic social tasks that society requires. These individuals will be able to do uncomplicated educational tasks involving reading, writing, speaking, listening, and some simple mathematic computations. We often call these people educable.

Those individuals who can only perform tasks at a pre-formal educational developmental stage are often called severely, profoundly, mentally retarded. Many subnormal individuals whom educators classify as trainable may fall into this particular group although some can progress into the formal educational developmental stage. Primary emphasis is to help these children develop their independent living and social skills so that they may live in society. The schools are required to provide services for all subnormally functioning individuals whether they can or cannot reach formal educational development.

Mental subnormal intelligence is characterized by a below average rate of functioning with the individual's chronological age group. This includes developmental growth, social living adjustment, and learning. Under the law it is defined by the term mental retardation. It states:

"Mentally retarded means significantly subaverage general intellectual functioning existing concurrently with deficits in adaptive behavior and manifested during the developmental period, which adversely affects a child's educational performance."

Mental Integration

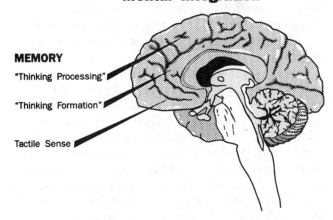

MEMORY

"Thinking Processing"

"Thinking Formation"

Tactile Sense

Mental Subnormality Terminology

ACQUIRED
Conditions due to influences that occurred after conception, such as accident, disease, birth injuries

AMBIDEXTROUS
Equally skilled use of either hand in activities

AMENTIA
Means mental retardation

ASPHYXIANT NEONATORUM
Oxygen deprivation of the newborn

ATTENTION SPAN
The amount of time concentration can be expected of an individual

AUTOSOME
Any paired chromosome other than the sex chromosomes

AUTOSOME DOMINANT GENE
In a paired chromosome situation, it is the gene that produces its effect on the contrasting chromosome

AUTOSOME RECESSIVE GENE
In a paired chromosome situation, it is the gene that fails to produce its effect on the contrasting chromosome

BACTEREMIA
Blood poisoning

BIRTH INJURY
Trauma occurrence during the birth process

BIRTH TRAUMA
Injury occurred during the birth process

BRAIN DAMAGE
Structural brain injury

BRAIN STEM
Brain axis between the spinal cord and the cerebellum which affects the motor sensory tract

CHROMOSOME
One of forty-six small masses within the cells which contain genes

CHROMOSOME FRAGMENTATION
The breaking up or parts becoming lost, misaligned, or translocated of the chromosomes

CONGENITAL
Being born with

CORTEX
Outside portion of the cerebrum

CYTOGENETICS
The formal study of hereditary characteristics of the genes and chromosomes

DEVELOPMENTAL DISABILITY
A handicap that's origin is found during the period of growth

DYSLOGIA
Impairment of thought processes

EDUCABLE MENTALLY RETARDED
An educational classification of those individuals whose IQ falls between 50-70 to 75

ENDOGENOUS
Of internal origin

ENZYME
A biochemical substance found in the body to stimulate a body change

EUGENICS
Formal study on improving hereditary characteristics

EXOGENOUS
Of external origin

GENE
The basic unit within a chromosome

HETEROCHROMOSOME
Sex chromosome

HORMONE
A glandular substance carried by the blood affecting performance of an organ

INTELLIGENCE
A measurement of a human being's ability to perceive, understand, and adapt to his or her environment.

LATERALITY
Preferred use pertaining to one side of the body

MALFORMATION
Defects accompanying improper physical development

MENTAL AGE
Intellectual level designated in test scores corresponding to chronological age

MENTAL DETERIORATION
Intellectual functioning that deteriorates or regresses

MENTAL HANDICAP
Mental retardation

MINIMAL BRAIN DAMAGE
Minor damage of the central nervous system

MUTATION
A change in a gene's orientation

NORMAL
Agreed upon standard of functioning

PRENATAL
Birth process involving time just prior to birth

PSYCHOGENIC
Origins are in the psychological system

RECESSIVE GENE
A gene which fails to perform its function on the contrasting gene

SEVERELY AND PROFOUNDLY HANDICAPPED
Mentally retarded individuals whose IQ falls below 25 according to education

TOXEMIA
Toxic substances that are part of the blood

TRAINABLE MENTALLY RETARDED
An educational term classifying individuals whose IQ falls between 25-50

TRAUMA
Injury

X-LINKED GENE
X chromosome found in the gene

SPECIFIC MENTAL SUBNORMAL FUNCTIONING

Incidental Involvement

INCIDENTAL ERRORS

Many students fall into the formal education area of subnormal mental deficiency because of lack of motivation. The advantages of an education in the classroom appear too difficult to attain and unrealistic. Many minority groups find the current educational system inappropriate because of social customs and language barriers.

Where children are physically and emotionally abused, learning processes may be blocked by emotional behavior resulting in either withdrawal or aggressiveness. Many simply can't keep their mind on their work.

Severely culturally deprived children often have had an inadequate or improper diet that may result in permanent damage to the human organism itself; hence they may have formal educational problems that result in their falling into the mental subnormal functioning level. Motivation, cultural values, and proper physical/emotional growth are three factors resulting in the lowering of intellectual functioning.

AUTISM

Subnormal functioning behavior that is related directly to autistic functioning behavior. Although psychological testing will show that the majority of children classified as autistic range in this handicapping category, the primary problem is believed to be a speaking and language difficulty with little or no verbal communication.

Since many of the available intelligence testing scales deal with oral and written communication measurements, autistic children will score poorly and hence receive subnormal intelligence classifications. Additional complications that influence this classification are the behavior patterns that accompany autism, which also conversely affect the poor performance given on an individual psychological examination.

Because of low mental functioning ability, one would conclude that these children cannot achieve higher level academic performance and thinking skills. When working intensely with these individuals, many high level performance thinking and learning skills are exhibited. Special emphasis of instruction should be placed on the communication skills.

CEREBRAL PALSY
(Neurological Problems)

The cerebral palsied victim embraces a neurological impairment that occurs in the brain and/or central nervous system. Because of this damage, many exhibit the range of mental subnormal functioning. Depending upon the amount of neurological damage, the amount of intellectual ability available for learning and thinking to take place will vary. This varying factor determines whether we will include the cerebral palsied victim in the educational programming involving both preformal and formal education with the subnormal mental functioning group. Handicapping conditions involving the neurological system may exhibit similar type behaviors. See categories under the physically handicapped for those individuals whose handicaps are classified under neurological conditions.

DEAFNESS

Young deaf children's failure to obtain language through sound often makes them test in the subnormal mental ability range. This is mainly due to their inability to score well on language-type activities included on an individual intelligence test. Because language directly influences mental capacity, subnormal performance scores may occur.

SEVERE EMOTIONALLY DISTURBED

Behavior patterns involving those individuals who exhibit extreme withdrawal tendencies may influence mental functioning ability. This withdrawal suggests upon the part of the individual an inability to communicate formally or informally. This extreme withdrawal behavior may be mistaken for severe neurological damage that accompanies many types of mental subnormality. In many cases the physical manifestations are almost identical and need to be explored by a neurological examination before a decision is made as to what type of educational assistance is needed.

ACQUIRED APHASIA

Mental subnormal functioning may be present after the aphasic condition occurs in the individual. Generally, this handicapping disappears as the person recovers. Permanency of inferior subnormal functioning occurs due to the amount of neurological damage incurred. Aphasic victims have difficulty in integrating mental skills. Because of the language and communication problems, we realize the importance of subjective interpretation of psychological testing for mental functioning at both the preformal and formal level.

HYPERKINETIC BEHAVIOR SYNDROME

Overactive children display many of the same characteristics found with those functioning at a subnormal mental level. They have short attention spans, are easily distracted, and often frustrated. Many have behavior patterns similar as well, which include fidgety, restless, impulsive, and quarrelsome natures. It is important that diagnosis be considered before placing this type of child in an educational setting where learning is presented at a slower rate. This "minimal brain dysfunction" defect, no matter how complex and how disruptive to school type tasks, does not necessarily equate itself with mental subnormal intelligence.

Functional Involvement

Mental Ability Classification
Comparative Terminology in Mental Retardation

American Psychiatric Association (PSM-111)	IQ Level
Mild Mental Retardation	50-70
Moderate Mental Retardation	35-49
Severe Mental Retardation	20-34
Profound Mental Retardation	Below 20
Unspecified Mental Retardation	-

American Assoc. on Mental Deficiency (ICD-9) (Grossman, 1983)	IQ Level
Mild Mental Retardation	50-55 to Approx. 70
Moderate Mental Retardation	34-40 to 50-55
Severe Mental Retardation	20-25 to 35-40
Profound Mental Retardation	Below 20 or 25
Unspecified Mental Retardation	-

Educational Classification Used by School System	IQ Level
Educable Mentally Retarded (EMR)	50-70 or 75
Trainable Mentally Retarded (TMR)	25-50
Severely/Profoundly Handicapped (SPH)	Below 25

Educational Classification Used by Most School Systems

EDUCABLE MENTALLY RETARDED

The educable mentally retarded have an approximate IQ of 50-70. The mental subnormal functioning level is the result of socioeconomic and/or genetic conditions. They are expected to achieve academically from the third to sixth grade level in the public school setting. Special adaptations for an appropriate education are necessary largely through a resource teacher. Their adaptive behavior (personal independence and social ability to interact with both peers and society) may require direct instruction with many direct experiences. They are capable of learning unskilled semi-skilled work. They can also meet the social demands imposed upon them.

Physically, the educable mentally retarded individual is slightly below average in weight or height. His major difference is that he has moderate physiological defects which increase the chance for functioning at a subnormal level. These physiological defects are largely concerned with sensory-motor areas (visual, auditory, kinesthetic (gross and fine motor skills)). Language and speech development is sometimes poor.

TRAINABLE MENTALLY RETARDED

The trainable mentally retarded have an approximate IQ of 24-49. The mental subnormal functioning level results from a wide variety of neurological, glandular or metabolic defects or disorders that are generally rare. Academic range of functions vary from total non-academic learning to achieving educational functioning to a second grade level. As their label states, these children can be trained in self-care and social adjustment skills. Their adaptive behaviors are as difficult for these children to achieve as their academic level of functioning. As adults they tend to be found in sheltered workshop conditions where they remain under constant supervision. Special emphasis in needed in their social development and the treatment of them as functioning individuals in society.

PROFOUNDLY MENTALLY RETARDED

The profoundly mentally retarded have IQ's below 25. The mental subnormal functioning level is the result of rare neurological, glandular, or metabolic defects or disorders. Training is useful in self-care and self-help skills. Constant nursing or supervisory care is required.

Prenatal/Infant Variables

General Variables

Mental retardation's origin is often times unknown. The greatest number of people affected with mutual retardation have chromosome abnormalities. Chemical disorders where inborn errors of metabolism may affect the functioning of the brain. Phenylketonuria and Hunters syndrome are examples of such deficiencies. Malformation of the nervous system which influences the brain itself may result in subnormal intelligence. Hydrocephalus, spina bifida and anencephaly are structural irregularities in the nervous system. Links between blood groups and mental retardation have been established through the incompatibility of blood types. This is known as the R-H factor which can be tested and treated to prevent mental retardation. Birth can create harmful effects on the brain forcing brain damage to occur. Breech delivery cuts off the flow of oxygen to the brain at the perinatal stage, and certain drugs taken during delivery may cause brain hemorrhage. The quality of prenatal care under a medical doctor's supervision is a protection against many birth defects leading to mental retardation.

Genetic Disorders

Genetic Counseling

Genetic counseling conveys understanding of birth defects by providing and interpreting medical information based on the knowledge of human genetics. Childbearing decision making can be made to prospective parents. Genetic counselors can predict the probability of recurrence of a given abnormality for a married couple. The prediction is based on the basic laws governing hereditary as well as the knowledge of frequency of specific birth defects in a given population.

Normal development and functioning of every living organism depends on genetic information transmitted by the male and female at the moment of conception. Inborn characteristics or traits are controlled by the action of one or more pairs of genes (one-half male, one-half female) containing chromosomes within the nucleus of all body cells. In each chromosome there are literally hundreds of genes. Among this vast number of genes, abnormality may be found. These abnormal genes potentially cause body deformities or defects.

Chromosomal defects are or may be affected in a specific pregnancy. Cells composing all organisms contain a fixed number of chromosomes in pairs. In humans there are 23 named pairs or a total of 46 chromosomes per cell. In the reproductive cells (sperm and ovum) each contains 23 unpaired chromosomes. A reproductive cell is provided by the male and female at conception. As they fuse into one cell a full chromosome count results.

Chromosomal errors occur in the reproductive cell formation, hence a number of abnormal chromosomes may be present. This abnormality is repeated into millions of cells in the growing embryo affecting both body functions and structures.

Information concerning specialized genetic services is available through the March of Dimes. *An International Directory of Genetic Services* is a complete compilation which is available from most doctors and other medical professionals.

This publication lists over 250 mentally retarded syndromes identified by medical and chemical research.

The following genetic defects are transmitted as follows:

Autosomal dominant - Trait is inherited from one parent and from the previous generation

Recessive inheritance - Both parents are affected

X-linked inheritance - Sex-linked when the gene for the characteristic is known to be on the X chromosome

Multifactorial inheritance patterns - Any combination of the above-listed factors.

Acrochpalo Syndrome (Apert's Syndrome) (Autosomal Dominant)
Mental Retardation-special education needed, skeletal abnormalities, facial abnormalities.

Ataxia (Louis-Bar) (Autosomal Recessive)
Mental retardation-special education needed, eye deficiencies in movement, may affect any extremity area.

Juvenile Amaurotic (Idiocy) (Autosomal Recessive)
Intellectual deterioration begins at 5 to 7 years of age-death at 14 to 17 years of age.

Amsterdam Syndrome (Autosomal Recessive)
Severely retarded, facial deformities.

Cri-du-Chat Syndrome (Short Arm of #5)
Severe mental retardation if survives.

Crouzon's Disease (Autosomal Dominant)
Mental retardation-mild to moderate, facial abnormalities.

Deletion 18 Long Arm Syndrome (Long arm of #18)
Severe mental retardation.

Deletion 18 Short Arm Syndrome (Short arm of #18)
Severe mental retardation

Down's Syndrome (Chromosome #21)
Severe to moderate retardation, facial and body deformities.

Edward's Syndrome (Chromosome #18)
Severe mental retardation, organ malformation possibilities.

Fragile X (Long arm of X chromosome)
Severe mental retardation.

Freidreich's Atavia (Autosomal dominant/recessive)
Mental retardation present, onset at 6 to 8 years of age, progressively fatal.

Fructosemia (Autosomal Recessive)
Possible mental retardation-liver malfunction.

Galactosemia (Autosomal Recessive)
Mental retardation if not treated-metabolic disorder.

Hartnup's Syndrome (Autosomal Recessive)
Mild to moderate retardation-neurological damage.

Huntington's Chorea (Autosomal Dominant)
Seven to ten years-mental retardation in final stages.

Hydrocephalus (Y-linked recessive)
Mental retardation-varies in severity-visual/auditory defects.

Klinefelter's (XXY sex chromosome)
Mental retardation with special education needed-sterility.

Laurence-Moon-Biedl Syndrome (Autosomal Recessive)
Mental retardation with special education needed, dwarfism, visual problems.

Lesch-Nyhan (X-linked recessive gene)
Mental retardation-with special education-metabolic disorder.

Maple Syrup Urine Disease (Autosomal Recessive)
Neurological damage possible-mental retardation.

Marfan's Syndrome (Autosomal Dominant)
Organs of the body irregular-possible retardation-orthopedic problems.

Microcephaly (Autosomal recessive-possible X-linked)
Moderate to profound mental retardation, small in body size, possible convulsions.

MPS I Hurler's Syndrome (Autosomal Recessive)
Mental retardation-enlarged head with irregular features.

MPS II Hurler's Syndrome (X-linked recessive)
Mental retardation-enlarged head with irregular features.

MPS III Sanfilippo Syndrome (Autosomal Recessive)
Mental retardation-with special education assistance-irregular head features.

Neurofibromatosis (Autosomal Recessive)
Mental retardation-with special education assistance-tumors.

Niemann-Pick (Autosomal Dominant)
Mental retardation-blindness-death before 3 years of age.

Patau's Syndrome (Chromosome #13)
Mental retardation-life support maintenance.

Pelizaeus-Merzbacher (X-linked recessive)
Mental retardation-death by 6 years of age.

Phenylketonuria (PKU) (Autosomal recessive gene)
Mental retardation-if not treated-neurological disorders.

Parder-Will (Genetic-possible)
Mild to moderate mental retardation.

Retts Syndrome (Unknown-possible X-linked chromosome)
Mental retardation-epilepsy-motor skill deficiencies.

Tay-Sachs (Autosomal Recessive)
Mental retardation-convulsions.

Tuberous Sclerosis (Autosomal Dominant)
Mental retardation varies-organ disorders.

Turner's Syndrome (X chromosome)
Possible mental retardation-sterility, irregular body structure.

Waardenburg Syndrome (Autosomal Dominant)
Possible mental retardation-with special education needed.

Wilson's Disease (Autosomal Recessive)
Normal early development then gradual intellectual decline, emotional problems.

FUNCTIONAL ERRORS

PRE-FORMAL EDUCATION

Those individuals who have limited ability are very dependent upon the adults in their environment. These severe and profound mentally handicapped individuals, described as non-verbal, have limited self-care skills, and have minimal socially adaptive behaviors. Many multiple handicapped individuals fall into this category because of one or more severe disabilities such as deafness, blindness, or motor problems.

Special emphasis is being made to train teachers and other auxiliary personnel to help these special people to learn. They will take a particular task (going to the bathroom on time) and help the student slowly, step-by-step to plan a method whereby the severe/profound handicapped individual can control this social skills behavior. Many self-help skills, social skills, and even verbal skills can be learned by giving this child special attention. Planned experiences such as the Special Olympics help all of us to better realize the specialness that these people can bring and how they can touch the heart of all who take these needs for granted.

Pre-Formal Education Checklist

Mental Integration
- Recognize similarities
- Recognize differences
- Identify objects in pictures
- Solve a real life problem (carry tray to seat)
- Make a judgement in common sense situation (wear a coat)
- Reason out simple real life situation (why we are quiet in the hot lunch room)

Perceptual (visual/auditory)
- Attend to a visual stimuli (mother, father)
- Follow a moving object
- Fixate eyes on object
- Discriminate between 2 objects
- Know whole/part relationships
- Recall a visual description of an item
- Attend to loud noise
- Know sound differences
- Detect sounds in relation to distance
- Reproduce a sound
- Reproduce (words, sentences, etc.)

Perception (tactile/kinesthetic)
- Examine an object through touch
- Identify an object while holding it
- Match objects by moving them in close proximity

Social
- Awareness of family members
- Ability to be recognized
- Play appropriately
- Stay within requested limits
- Follow directions
- Realize social behavior appropriate to a social situation
- Organize activities

Language
- Use receptive language (understand commands)
- Use expressive language (describe a need)
- Read functional words (men/women, walk, wait)
- Write simple words (name, address, phone)
- Use phone
- Communicate in purchase of necessities (grocery store, restaurant)

Self Help
- Perform toileting procedures
- Can feed/eat/drink independently
- Groom self (wash hands, face; comb hair, apply deodorant)
- Oral hygiene (teeth)
- Nasal hygiene (blow nose, use a tissue)
- Clothing care (dress/undress, maintain clothing)
- Personal safety (know danger, pedestrian skills)
- Independent skills (be able to put on/take off any clothing item)
- Make choices in home and family living
- Simple community responsibilities
- Act independently

Motor Skills
- Gross motor development (control body extremities, maintain balance, move total body)
- Fine motor development (use hands, reach, grasp, eye/hand movements)

FORMAL EDUCATION

There are mentally subnormal individuals who develop at a below average rate and experience difficulty in learning academic tasks as well as have adaptive behaviors and social adjustment difficulties.

These mentally retarded individuals can learn and perform in the regular school environment with special assistance. This special assistance needed involves basic thinking and learning situations which deal with awareness (perception), attention, and memory.

Thinking processes that relate to organizing/rehearsing receptive stimuli, concept formation and mental cognition skills need to be taught in the academic school classroom. Learning integration skills dealing with application of concepts learned, such as problem-solving, in the social and academic school setting with individuals of a similar chronological age group.

Formal Education Checklist

Memory
· Poor expressive language
· Poor receptive language skills
· Remembers events happening long ago but not recent events
· Difficulty in memorizing rhymes/poems

Concepts
· Little imagination
· Slow responses
· No sense of humor
· Expressionless
· Difficulty with relationships
   Yesterday, today, one year ago
   Likenesses/differences between objects
   Classification of objects
· Cannot associate logical sequences
   "If I _____, then I will _____."
· Fails to read a social situation
· Thinking inability:
   Trouble with logical sequence
   Trouble with different emotional expressions
   Trouble making up/telling a story

Academic Problems
· Difficulty in following directions
· Difficulty with rules of the classroom
· Can't ignore distractions
· Has trouble completing a task/assignment
· Trouble with group activity participation
· Accepting ideas of peers/teacher
· Recognizing feeling of other
· Trouble with refusing
· Difficulty in dealing with angry persons

Speaking
· Trouble describing picture, object
· Trouble responding orally to a question
· Difficulty with completing open-ended sentences
· Unresponsive when participation in a conversation/discussion is required
· Has difficulty in oral reading activities
· Written assignments are poor in quality
· Clumsy in handling books, small items
· Cutting, drawing are of poor quality
· Writing of reversals is found in written assignments
· Finds tracing through mazes difficult
· Tying shoe laces, buttoning coat is laborious

Spelling
· Has trouble putting the sound and symbol together
· Errors are made in reversals of letter in a word
· Difficulty in seeing/realizing a whole word
· Difficulty in transposing correct spelling of words in writing assignments
· Failure to include endings (-ed, -s, -ing, etc.) in spelling
· Difficulty in finding spelling errors in words

Reading
· Confusion with similar letters
   (b and d, o and e, b and p, r and u, h and k)
· Words misread when they have similar form (said and sand, then and the, you and yes)
· Inability to organize letters
· Reversals are common (was for saw, no for on, tap for pat)
· Knows letter sound one day and not the next
· Can't hear sound differences (vowel sounds that

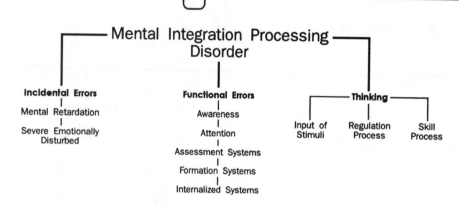

Mental Integration Processing Disorder

Incidental Errors	Functional Errors	Thinking
Mental Retardation	Awareness	Input of Stimuli
Severe Emotionally Disturbed	Attention	Regulation Process
	Assessment Systems	Skill Process
	Formation Systems	
	Internalized Systems	

2. MENTAL INTEGRATION PROCESSING

THINKING ACTIVITY FORMATION/DELIVERY SYSTEM

Mental Integration Terminology

Mental integration is not a direct category identifiable under P.L. 94-142 requiring direct services. Many learning disabled persons exhibit problems that directly relate to an inability to assess and process academic tasks. These individuals are covered under the educational mandate that assistance be made available to them. This category is referred to under the law as specific learning disabilities.

Mental integration functioning involves the total learning process. It begins when the stimuli are appropriately processed perceptually.

It's major responsibility occurs in the brain itself where integrational functioning takes place. Thinking both regulates and combines/connects information. Mental integration processing is complete when that information can be transmitted accurately in spoken or written symbols. Specific difficulties relating to those problems that may cause an individual to be incapable of performing appropriate academic, social, or emotional tasks will be addressed. No attempt is being made to develop a theory for how intellectual mental functioning (cognition) occurs. This current topic is being studied and theorized with different philosophies being developed. Problems and deficiencies manifested in this area are frequent and identifiable. Attempts to identify the problem with some background information for the reader are being considered.

The area of the brain and how it functions is mysteriously unique especially when considering each human being individually. This writer has limited background in how the brain receives, internalizes, and transmits stimuli, and does not plan to attempt to cover such a complicated and complex subject.

Mental Integration

Cognition
The ability to use high level thinking and learn independently.

Domain knowledge
The concepts necessary to have command of a content area (social studies, reading).

Learning strategy
A plan that attempts to understand a concept, idea, in a systematic way.

Mental cognition
The person's ability to think about his/her own learning.

Schema
A system of concepts.

Skill
A learned ability to perform a task.

Sequence
A series of steps required to solve a problem or a skill.

Problem
A question, puzzle, disagreement, or need.

Solution
A response, outcome, or result.

Compare
Resembles; things in common.

Contrast
Differences, on the one hand, if . . . then.

Concept
Relationship, category, connection, set.

Description
What things appear, seem, illustration, shows, furthermore.

Thinking
A symbolic transformation of stimuli (sensory data).

Memory
A set of abstract skills.

Creativity
The conception of a new and original response.

Stimuli

Idea or imagery found in life's experiences of the environment.

Image

Call up of a mental picture.

Checklist

MEMORY

· Difficulty remembering what is heard (words, sentences, directions)
· Doesn't pay attention to directions in classroom
· Has trouble identifying words with similar sequence (days of the week)
· Confuses words
· Poor comprehension skills in reading
· Understands a word but cannot retrieve it for practical use
· Remembers a word but cannot retrieve it for practical use
· Remembers things happening long ago but not recently
· Cannot recall a previous learned concept after a given period of time
· Makes same error continuously
· Poor spelling skills

MENTAL INTEGRATION

· Fails to see relationships (objects, situation)
· Little original imagination
· Trouble with "what happens next" type of activities
· Difficulty with comparing likeness/differences type situations
· Can't read a social situation
· Can't associate a particular act with the consequence
· Trouble creating a story
· Difficulty with a pun or joke
· Has trouble with time sequences

Decision Making/Problem Solving

1. What feelings relate to the problem?
2. What is the actual problem (write it in own words)?
3. What is the goal?
4. Think of ways to get to goal.
5. Think of the consequences each plan might have.
6. Decide which plan is best for you.
7. Precede with going through with your plan, even with the roadblocks that lie ahead.

MENTAL INTEGRATION

Incidental Involvement

INCIDENTAL ERRORS

MENTAL RETARDATION

Mental retardation is defined as having subnormal intellectual functioning and impairment of adaptive behavior with people of a similar chronological age group. Measurement is designated through formal psychological testing. Levels of achievement are expressed in terms of pre-formal and formal educational levels.

Failure to accommodate complex mental integration processing is common. Perception-motor problems, difficulty with awareness, attention and memory processing are deficiencies observed. The skilled use of thinking skills relating to problem solving and critical thinking is seldom reached. Mentally subnormal conditions exhibit many of the deficiencies found in mental integration problems, but mental subnormal functioning should not be considered as the same condition as mental integration processing.

SEVERE EMOTIONAL PROBLEMS

Severe emotionally disturbed children are measured primarily in terms of emotional and behavioral difficulties. Behavior is described in terms of extreme or unacceptable by social or cultural standards. No measurement tool is precise enough to design such a label. Mental integration processing problems can be or are the by-product of the abnormal functioning level exhibited by the emotionally disturbed. Attention deficit characteristics are particularly observed. Memory and awareness deficits are known to exist. The output or expression of ideas often shows patterns of irregularity, incoherence, and mental subnormality. Mental integration processing is important to improving the condition of the emotionally disturbed child. It is neither the cause of nor the same as the serious emotionally disturbed category under P.L. 94-142.

Functional Involvement

FUNCTIONAL ERRORS

AWARENESS

Inability to consistently recognize or become confused in responding to something is a major mental integration problem. Awareness of objects or situations such as dress, room design, or a city plan is basic for good mental processing to occur. Basic awareness also includes a consciousness in shape, size, color, and overall design of objects and structures.

When consistent patterns of awareness exist, failure to respond will deter the foundation of developing mental concepts. Attending to what a speaker says in conversation or on the phone and giving an appropriate response is important. Appreciation for, or a sensitivity to objects or situations with appropriate responses is a necessary foundation for the thinking skill process to proceed as intended. Withdrawal will take over if responsive awareness fails to mature.

ATTENTION

Attention deals with stimuli in the immediate present. This requires the individual's desire to become involved in or committed to a particular situation or activity where he or she will seek out and engage in that particular appropriate form of behavior.

Responding requires: a willingness or ability to adjust to the needed behavior; the capacity for voluntary choice and selection of the behavior; and the enjoyment or appreciation of the response selected.

Mental integration problems may become apparent when this process is interrupted. Problems that might interrupt the mental ability for attention may need special consideration. The inability to focus on a particular stimulus, both verbally or nonverbally, is possible. A failure to withdraw his attention from a particular object or situation (perseverance) could be observed. Discriminating between important and unimportant stimuli may deter the attending process. When this problem becomes consistent, an overwhelming emotional fear grips the individual.

ASSESSMENT SYSTEMS

Consideration of or attending to factors, viewpoint, situation, and objects is an important process in the internalization of information used by the brain (terminal for mental integration/processing). Assessment is based on the consistency of repeated use of responses. This consistency is called a value or belief. The major criterion used by the individual is called the worth of the response(s) needed. Internalization of a value or belief may be assessed as mere acceptance or a firm conviction which influences its position in the thought process.

Conceptual difficulties arise when newly assisted information cannot be retrieved. The fragmentation of either new or old information may cause a great deal of difficulty. In the academic setting. Special emphasis must be placed on activities used in the development of short and long term memory processing.

FORMATION SYSTEM

The brain is the center where selected stimuli enter, to become internalized. The internalization process involves the formulation of a new, appropriate and more accurate informational system. This requires an organizational process which determines the relationship between present systems with new information being brought into the brain for changing or altering a given condition or idea. Abstract, symbolic, and verbal internalization of stimuli result in the formation of a more accurate, useful idea or behavior.

Organization and formation of new concepts, ideas, or behaviors may also be difficult for children having difficulty in mental integration processing. Problems may arise when the individual cannot find the most appropriate stimulus. Finding differences between two stimuli to organize a new idea or behavior may be difficult to establish.

Problem solving through practical and constructive thinking may require considerable attention when difficulties arise in this area. Impulsive decision-making problems may be addressed by providing concrete experiences where good judgement elements may be modeled and explained.

INTERNALIZED SYSTEM

The internalized system finds the individual functioning at the level where there is the system toward attitudes and values at that particular moment. This generalized basic set enables a person to function with regularity when judging issues, situations, and consequences. By realizing the functioning of the system within the individual, one is able to characterize the individual as he functions in his environment.

Internalized systematic defects to observe are memory deficits, defective comprehension, improper abstract concepts, and problems in verbal communication. One must realize the importance of how abstract concepts are related to language itself; that through the language process, logical relationships and/or analogies are expressed accurately. If inadequate intellectual activity is not taking place, new concepts and thinking and logical deductions become disorganized, idiosyncratic, and unfruitful.

THINKING ACTIVITY

The brain to the body is much like a terminal in a large airport. It is the center of all information requiring mental processing. It is responsible for the receiving and processing of stimuli as an airport receives passengers from various airlines and sends them through various passageways. New information is permitted just as passengers are discharged to their desired destinations.

The nervous system is the passage way that both receives and emits images. As the airlines deliver their planes, and hence their passengers, to, through, and out of the terminal, so does the nervous system collect and integrate stimuli to eventually emit information from the individual him/herself.

As you travel by air, you find that many factors exercise how well the process is completed. Planes fail to meet arrival and departure times. Luggage gets lost in the terminal. The distance in the terminal between one airline and another is too far to connect in a given framework of time. The gates may post a wrong sign. It may be difficult to hear the arrival or departure of a particular flight. The constant motion and movement involved in that environment becomes disturbing. Or you may not be aware of the complexity and difficulty of the environment that controls the terminal and simply give up flying as a means of transportation. Because of the complexity of the process and your personal being in relationship to that process, a difficulty may occur.

The body is much like an airport. It requires a receptive system (visual, auditory, tactile), passageway (nervous system), a terminal (brain), and a way of departure (speech/language/motion, movement). When all systems are functioning, the process works! When any of the above fail to function, the mental processing is disrupted or fails.

The brain has a structure of two hemispheres (parts). These hemispheres are thought of as the right and left side of the brain. Each hemisphere has specialized terminal centers where the nervous system sends its specialized response. The brain itself is a lobed organ that is composed of grey matter cells. This system has many blood vessels from the circulation system in its structure which provide constant oxygen and food for cellular composition and construction. The brain (terminal) itself has its own regulatory and mechanical needs which complicate the mental integration processing system. When the brain mechanically fails the mental functioning is sure of being affected. This influences any or all manifestations considered in this book.

The brain functions in a constant state of motion or movement. It is responsive to many different types of movement at one time which requires immediate attention and processing called thinking.

Thinking is both a regulation process and skill. It operates a system of events and thus influences the direction that produces new information. Cognition is sometimes used for this term but for simplicity the term "thinking," which is familiar to all, will be used.

Functional Involvement
INPUT OF STIMULI

The brain is the center of the internalization process. It receives the incoming stimuli in order for thinking processes to function. It relies on the individual's environmental life system for the knowledge needed to perform. Major difficulties in mental integration processing take place when the individual fails to stimulate ideas from the person and when life environment experiences fail to enhance him/herself as a being.

The organization of an environmental life system is dependent on the physical body, social self, and life environment.

The physical body is a flexible, energy filled organism or being. Its development is dependent on space and movement. The fundamental body processes responsible for its proper functioning in space are the visual, auditory, and haptic (tactile and kinesthetic) sensory systems which perceive stimuli and send those stimuli messages to be internalized by the brain. For a good transmission system to function, these body processes should all be functioning.

Movement controls the source of knowledge. It is the mechanism that regulates all basic human experience. Movement controls the acts of the body and how it interrelates to its environment. It controls the function of thinking. Movement is the source of all learning that relates to the body. When the motor system that relates to movement fails to function, the mental integration processes will fail to mechanically perform.

The brain's ability to receive stimuli for internalizing depends upon the body and how it functions as a social being. Communication involves the speech and thought processes. Socialization involves learning (instructional) patterns and cultural patterns.

Communication is a form of body movement that is based upon the though relationship between adults or peers alike. Speech is the mechanical production that expresses communication.

Communication is dependent upon the thought relationship developed through speech and its movement patterns. When appropriate speech, hence also communication patterns, fail to develop an internalizing process problem exists.

Ideas and images that are being sent to the brain are being producing via the socialization process. This social self involves both movement and thought.

Thought is embedded in the history of the person and is reflective of natural cultural patterns. Early cultural patterns that influence such images might be trauma, loss of a parent, or having been abused as a child. Feelings become an interweaving web in the body and in how it functions and perceives its space. Processing receiving stimuli by the brain may be influenced by movement in the life environment of that individual. It is the ability to comprehend and experience space. Infants actively approach their environment. Concretely, they are conjuring the raw material of vision by the process of single glances. Impressions and images are developed through the selection, organization, and interpretation of these visible components. These eventually develop vocabulary (hence language) which is internalized into thought. This is a very detailed process.

Symbolically, the concrete visuals and images can be elaborated. Through perceived relationships in myth, art, religion, and education the concrete approach has been elevated to higher levels of thought. This is useful when learning integrative skills related to thinking, such as problem solving and initial thinking which are becoming a part of the integration of mental process.

Failure on the part of the individual's inability to develop the necessary awareness patterns of experiencing and moving through his life environment results in difficulties in the internalization of processing that takes place in the brain itself. When concrete and symbolic life experiences are not actively pursued, deficits in thinking processing occur.

Mental Integration Processing
THINKING (as a Regulation Process)

The internalization of sensory input for the production of new ideas and imagery or the reshaping of previous ideas or imagery involves a regulation process called thinking. Specific types of mental integration problems are characterized by difficulty in developing a new idea referred to as concept formation. Often various ideas (concepts) can be taught in isolation with meaning but reworking them for new information seems impossible, especially for those individuals functioning in the subnormal range of intelligence. In many cases this is difficult because of the inability to hold or retrieve an image or idea that is relevant to forming a different concept. The failure for these sets of skills to be effective is called memory loss or problems relating to recall. Thinking involves the processes and regulating of skills to formulate concepts through the use of memory. Memory involves the retrieving of relevant images and ideas for development and formation of a message or a skill that can be useful to the life environment of the body or social being. People vary in their thinking ability

because of the amount of desire or willingness to be involved in the pursuit of new ideas.

Mental Integration Processing
THINKING (as a Complex Skills Process)

Thinking is in full motion when a person's mind is integrating ideas, images, fact fragments with the content of his/her life environment. The ability to regenerate ideas and activities can be utilized effectively by the person. This is often referred to as high-order (level) thinking (cognition may be a substitute term).

When thinking as a complex skill is being internalized by the brain, routine type processing transforms into a complicated system. This thinking system utilizes such skills as making judgements, interpretations, multiple solutions, and applying multiple criteria for a solution. Many learning disabled individuals who have mental subnormal and severe emotional problems, and language difficulties have difficulty in obtaining this level of mental integration processing.

The mental integration processing of thinking as a complex skill requires the individual to connect information by combining two or more learned concepts. A step-by-step (sequencing) is necessary in complex skills such as problem solving, decision making, creative thinking, etc. Individual problems arise when the ability to perform these steps are lacking. When attempts are made to implement complex thinking skills these procedures need to be kept in mind.

More emphasis is being placed on school-aged children to have experiences in learning these complex integration processing skills. Problem solving, decision making and creative thinking are familiar forms of complex thinking that are being used.

Problem solving requires the ability to earn step-by-step plans to complete a task of resolving a difficulty. First, one needs to be aware of the exact difficulty. Second, one must make judgements as to possible actions that can be useful in solving the difficulty. Third, the selection process requires the use of cause/effort relationship skills. Fourth, the best plan of action is decided and employed. Possible difficulties for those having trouble with mental integration include keeping the plan of action when each step involves a thinking skill. Any step may also be difficult to complete. Common state, guessing, first solution selection, spoken or written response are presentative.

Decision making requires the skill for selection. Alternatives are given and the response is needed. Step-by-step procedure requires: first, the comprehension of a problem; second, the selection of the best alternative;

third, the formation of a response. Similar problem areas with realizing the step-by-step procedure that must be taken. The basic thinking skill of comprehension is an ever present nagging problem. Formulating the response requires oral and/or written expression which possesses additional difficulty.

Creative thinking requires novel and new ideas/ products. Original thinking which can best be explained in terms of a new creation or reevaluation. These steps are usually ill-defined and require abstract thinking and planning. The best descriptive term to use for those attempting this complex thinking skill who have mental integrative problems is "confused without response."

Attempts to create experiences and opportunity should be attempted. This is by far the most difficult handicap to overcome. If success can be made in this area, however, what a major triumph can be achieved.

Specific Types of Thinking Activity
OUTPUT OF IDEAS/IMAGERY

The brain's internalization combines the mental integration processing of stimuli (production of idea/ imagery) with the neurological system which leaves the brain appropriately for the required expression needed. Appropriate expressive modes include speech (oral, language, reading, and writing (spelling). The final product is measured by content, quality, and quantity.

Difficulties resulting from any mental integration delivery system are difficult to identify. Since the means of measurement is largely assessed by quantity and quality, it does not necessarily mean that the expressive system is malfunctioning; it could be the neurological system or the motor system. When papers are not completed, content is fragmented or poor on written assignments, and plagiarizing is persistent, then one should turn to oral responses. Type assignment to see if the pattern of work is similar. Content and quality in oral responses may be amazingly and pleasantly reversed. Oral responses are the best measurement of the quality and quantity of content, and are the required method of measurement under P.L. 94-142. The most consistent and best performance of expressive material is the most acceptable legally. There is no fundamental educational or legal exception that says that "written performance" is a requirement for life experiences and must be the required for measurement.

Structure is also a key to good mental process expression. Structure or discipline is an inward quality which pulls together the focus of thinking to create the needed product. It must be present at each step of both thinking regulation and complex skill processing. Emphasis on overcoming major mental integrative difficulties should include the development of inner controls so that needed quality and quantity of knowledge content can be properly expressed!

FUNCTIONAL ERRORS

CONCEPT FORMATION DIFFICULTIES

Concept formation is the ability to generate from past experiences of a similar nature a new set of ideas or images. It is a thinking outcome that is based on the brain's intellectual organic capacity and the number and variety of experiences experienced in the life environment.

Difficulty in the ability to develop a concept may vary depending on the nature of its complexity. Pre-formal educational types of life environmental needs include those ideas and skills necessary as a social being, involving objects, social experience, and abstract skills.

Objects: Tooth brush, car, fork, dog, etc.
Social experience: Restaurant dining, baseball game, trip to a mall, birthday party.
Abstract skills: Music, plays, justice, honor, respect.

Formal educational type of life experiences involve skills and ideas that generate personal and academic maturity. These concepts are specific and have well-defined boundaries. They include such things as:

Technical information (computer)
Scientific formal (cell)
Abstractions (religion)
Formal information (marriage, war)

Fundamental to all regulatory thinking processes is the skill of being able to formulate, understand, and use concepts. When individuals cannot functionally integrate this process, major academic and educational problems will persist.

MEMORY PROBLEMS

Memory is a set of skills that is essential for the brain's regulating process to function. Memory consists of a process called long term. Short term memory is an active on-going process that has a rapid forgetting rate. Short term memory transfers information by repeating that information over and over where it may be kept for immediate usage or transferred to long term memory for storage in the brain until it becomes necessary for retrieval. Long term memory has virtually an unlimited storage capacity. It is not easily disrupted like short term memory.

In the thinking process, memory is a much relied upon skill. When retrieval problems arise in long term memory, the thinking regulation process is significantly affected. This presents a major problem when confronted with the function of a concept or a skill needed by the expressive process.

Mental processing is currently beginning to be examined by many educators. For detailed and updated information contact:

U.S Department of Education
National Institute of Education
Educational Resources Information Center (ERIC)
555 New Jersey Ave NW
Washington D.C. 20208

SPECIFIC LEARNING DISABILITY

SPECIFIC LEARNING DISABILITY
A disorder in one or more of the basic psychological processes involved in understanding or in using language, spoken or written, which may manifest itself in an imperfect ability to listen, think, speak, read, write, spell, or to do mathematical calculations. The term includes such conditions as perceptual handicaps, brain injuries, minimal brain dysfunction, dyslexia, and developmental aphasia. The term does not include children who have learning problems which are primarily the result of visual, hearing, or motor handicaps, of mental retardation, of emotional disturbance, or of environmental, cultural, or economic disadvantage.
(As defined in the regulations for P.L. 94-142)

Specific Reading Difficulties ... Dyslexia

Mental Integration Processing Problem
Specific reading disorders are educational problems covering a broad range of reading skills from which specific causes have been identified. Dyslexia applies to a child who has difficulty learning to read for no apparent reason. Dyslexia shows a wide range of skills from identification of simple combinations of letters to comprehension and retention of material that has been read. Hyperlexics are those children who can read flawlessly passages containing complex words but have no idea of the meaning of the words they have read.

The basic skills involved in learning to read include:
Mental Integration Processing
· command of language
· left-right word/sentence orientation
· realizing spoken words are represented by print
· knowledge, reasoning, and evaluation of the printed word
Visual
· letter recognition
· letter discrimination

· the ability to recognize a printed word
  -the word itself
  -the word letters (morphones)
  -the letter sounds (phonones)
Auditory
· phonic orthographic pattern sounds
· sound-symbol correspondence

Reading is a mental integration processing (cognitive) skill that relies on long and short term memory processing as well as thinking skills that relate to processing information received. It relies heavily on receptive visual and auditory stimuli which produce images needed for the reading process to function properly. Educational, psychological, and biological causes have been cited as possible symptoms for the actual problem relating to a specific reading disability. Individual reading problems have been corrected by remediation in all of these areas and should be considered. The actual process of reading is complex and has many variables, any one of which could cause a specific problem.

Basic Vocabulary

WORD IDENTIFICATION SKILLS
the ability to recognize a given word by attacking it through the specific word's structure.

PICTURE CLUES
the ability to associate a given unfamiliar word when a picture illustration is given.

SIGHT WORDS
a list of basic words that have similar word patterns or configurations which are generally memorized (example: then, them, this)

PHONICS
association of sounds with the spoken word, analyze new words accordingly:
1. vowels/consonants
2. blends
3. combinations (vowels/consonants in varied positions)

WORD STRUCTURAL ANALYSIS
the ability to decode an unfamiliar word by finding root word, prefixes, suffixes, compound words, inflectional endings.

CONTEXT CLUES
the ability to recognize an unfamiliar word by reading the sentence, paragraph, and recognizing it through context meaning.

DICTIONARY USAGE
the ability to use the dictionary as a tool to identify phonic sounds that can produce the oral pronunciation of a word and ability to find a meaning of an unfamiliar word.

COMPREHENSION SKILLS

the ability to understand the written word.

VOCABULARY BUILDING

needs basic sight word vocabulary and knowledge of phonone and morphone sound patterns; develop vocabulary grouping of words by classifying (transportation, animals, clothes, states).

SENTENCE COMPOSITION

write simple sentences or stories, cut sentences in strips, give sentences for sequential arrangement, progress to longer, larger word, sentence composition.

STORY-PARAGRAPH MEANING

write formal story format (introduction, body, conclusion) - see *Reading, Writing: A Tutorial Guide in the Language Arts*, by Earl S. Zehr for lesson format.

LITERAL COMPREHENSION

the ability to understand the ideas and information explicitly stated in a passage (recall-main idea, detail, sequence, information)

INTERPRETATIVE COMPREHENSION

the ability to understand ideas and information inferred by a passage (reason/summarize).

CRITICAL COMPREHENSION

the ability to analyze, evaluate, and personally react to information presented in a passage (react/evaluate).

ORAL READING

the ability to enunciate a given word, sentence, or passage for the purpose of communicating meaning.

Checklist

Word Identification Checklist

· Recognize basic sight words
· Ability to sound out a given word
    -can recognize vowel sounds
    -can recognize consonant sounds
    -can utilize syllabication techniques
· Ability to analyze structure of a given word
    -can utilize syllable patterns in a given word
    -can locate root word
    -can locate prefixes
    -can locate suffixes
    -can locate inflectional endings
· Ability to use clues of context in attacking an unknown word
    -recognizes a definition clue
    -recognizes an experience clue
    -recognizes a comparison clue
    -recognizes a summarization clue

· Command of synonyms/antonyms
· Command of study skills (use of the dictionary as a word identification skills tool)

Comprehension Skills Checklist

· Commands a firm knowledge of meanings of words, sentences, paragraphs
· Ability to recall a main idea in a given passage
· Ability to give supportive ideas in a given passage
· Ability to recall a story sequence
· Ability to draw conclusions from given facts
· Ability to evaluate materials read
· Ability to relate reading to everyday situations
· Ability to use study skills information sources (table of contents, index, graphs, charts, maps)
· Ability to compare two story interpretations

Oral Reading Checklist

· Has good reading posture
· Has good word identification skills
· Can phrase meaningfully
· Can use punctuation symbols effectively
· Can identify key ideas
· Can read with fluency
· Can enunciate clearly
· Can convey feeling and meaning to audience

Incidental Involvement

Receptive stimuli including both visual and auditory reception may affect the ability to learn to read. Auditory reception is the inability to understand what is heard even though the hearing receptive organs are normal. Visual reception is the inability to understand what is seen even though the eyes are functioning normally. Distortion in both visual and auditory images may affect the ability to comprehend the written word and the symbol it represents. These may cause a specific reading problem.

Three broad categories are possible causes for specific reading problems:

Educational Involvement:

The task of learning to read is to link the spoken word with the written symbol. Various methods have been introduced to teach this task. Methods change from year to year by popular theories being introduced. The two major techniques used consistently include the whole-word approach and the phonetic approach. The whole-word approach views the words as units of whole symbolic units while the phonic approach introduces the letters and their sounds as they relate to the word unit.

Mental intelligence testing may cause educational measurement that is inaccurate. Since language and reading are key factors in intellectual measurement, inaccurate results may occur.

Psychological Disturbances:

Emotional stress may increase the possibility of having specific reading difficulties. This accompanying factor is considered more of an aggravating factor than a cause. Good emotional development and normal reading development go hand in hand. When a breakdown occurs deficiencies may become more pronounced.

Biological Involvement:

From psychological/physiological make-up stem specific reading problems including dyslexia. How this statement is interpreted varies. Neurologists believe the disorder occurs when mental integration functioning is abnormal. The functioning of the brain is organized abnormally or language areas of the brain are not clearly lateralized (dominance theory). These characteristics are frequently found in young children but as physical and mental growth patterns occur the organization and dominant functioning structure develops. Specific reading disabilities occur when these functions fail to develop properly.

Genetic factors link specific reading disabilities two ways. Males are six times more likely to have significant reading problems. Dyslexic reading problems are found in 40% of family histories.

Visual Perception Problems

Visual perceptual problems may be displayed in the child's handwriting performance. Reversals of letters such as (b,d: p,q: u,n) are frequented. Numbers are often reversed in position in math problems. Art work and drawings will be of poor quality as well.

Motor Expression

In manual type activities, displaying the skills relating to the manipulation of objects or pictures may produce more quality than lessons that require a great deal of handwriting. The disability inhibits such characteristics as body motions requiring any type of motor coordination such as walking, jogging, game activities involving the use of an object such as a ball). Tracing, drawing, and handwriting will also be affected.

Handwriting Agencies

American Association of Handwriting Analysis
820 W. Maple
Hinsdale, IL 60521

International Association of Master Penmen and Teachers of Handwriting
34 Broadway One
Ottawa, Ontario, Canada K15 2V6

International Graphoanalysis Society
111 N. Canal Street
Chicago, IL 60606

Functional Involvement

FUNCTIONAL ERRORS

Reading instruction is a complex mental integration process with many components. Strategies to teach reading have been implemented with varying degrees of success. No matter what reading instructional method is being taught, there are seven components that should be a part of an effective reading program found in educational setting designed for learning. Vocabulary, word recognition, comprehension, reading, physiology, content reading/skills, literary appreciation, and language patterning are components that aid the individual in unlocking the written form of the word. Neither program nor trained professional can teach an individual to read but both are merely helpful aides in guiding and promoting ways for that complex mental process to occur in the individual. Only the individual him/herself can decode or unlock the miracle of the most complex and required skill in the educational process.

Each component contributes to making the functioning of reading meaningful. Difficulties arise when a component has not effectively been introduced or mastered by the beginning reader. Reading instruction components are educationally introduced and reinforced in the first eight grades in school. Special instructions of a component vary as to the level at which it is taught in the elementary educational setting. The following descriptions may be helpful in understanding functional errors in reading.

VOCABULARY

Special vocabulary development is required for an individual to effectively understand any content of math, social studies, science, etc. By the time a student has reached grade seven, a command of over 8,500 words with a firm knowledge of their meaning should be acquired. Deficiency in the number of words known can greatly influence reading progress.

WORD RECOGNITION

The phoneme and morphone sound of each letter should be recognized for the purpose of unlocking the oral pronunciation of a given word. All word identification skills such as word structure analysis, context clues, dictionary usage to aid in word recognition and word meaning should be learned by the seventh grade level. Emphasis of this component is found in kindergarten, first and second grades.

COMPREHENSION

The ability to associate the written symbol with the ideas, object and actions is the heart of the reading-learning process.

READING PHYSIOLOGY

The ability to handle a book and physically position a book for easy and effective reading is a component that is taught. The formation of good reading habits makes the process comfortable and approachable.

CONTENT AREA/SKILLS

Each content area asks the reader to know its own vocabulary and the required skills necessary to comprehend the educational material involved. The skill of reading a graph, chemical formula, chart or map may be the ability to decode abbreviations found peculiar to that application. It may require symbols such as + for add, – for subtract, etc. These are called study skills and are included in all levels of the school program with special emphasis from third grade and up.

LITERARY APPRECIATION

An opportunity for enjoyment of all forms of the written words should be made available at all levels. This includes poetry, songs, short stories, magazines, periodicals, and full-length fiction and nonfiction books. Time in the school setting to be allotted for the child with a functional reading error will be reading with an emphasis placed on word recognition skills instead of literary appreciation. This robs the child of the most basic reading skill—the desire to enjoy the unlocking of the written word.

LANGUAGE PATTERNING

Consideration should be given to the language spoken in a given family or community versus a formal reading program. Do dialect and cultural differences impose a functional error in both the word recognition skills (particularly phonics) and comprehension skills? Serious consideration concerning individual program alternatives may need to be made to erase functional errors.

SPECIAL LEARNING DISABILITIES

SPELLING

Coordinating Skill

Spelling is the language art component that coordinates the network of its counterparts. To be an effective speller, one must have a fundamental knowledge of all language arts areas. Effective spelling is directly responsive to the phoneme-letter relationship; recognition of written letter form; formation of letter forms properly and legibly; and the development of automatic written communication responses. When all the other language arts skills are mastered, spelling skills will be easy to master.

Vocabulary List

PHONICS
a systematic approach used in reading and speaking which teaches the phonome-grapheme relationship.

PHONOME
a basic sound assigned to a given letter.

WORD
a composition of sounds.

ALPHABETIC LETTER
other written sound.

GRAPHEME
a written sound

SYLLABLE
a sound unit composed of one or more letters.

CORE VOCABULARY
selected word lists that are most used in society

SPELLING DEMONS
troublesome words that are persistently difficult for the general public to spell.

HOMONYMS
words spelled differently but having the same oral pronunciation.

TRANSPOSE
the tendency to reverse letters in a given word causing a spelling error.

WORD FORM
the visual alphabetic formation that gives a word a particular structure.

LETTER FORMATION
the ability to accurately form a given grapheme.

Checklist

· Can show a word form or image
· Recalls word spelling
· Word written carefully/legibly
· Can rhyme words
· Can enunciate sounds accurately
· Recognizes the concept of silent letters
· Recognizes syllables as word parts
· Understands capitalization rules necessary for accurate written word procedures
· Knows the concepts of prefixes, suffixes, and inflectional endings
· Recognizes a base word
· Has a firm command of synonyms, antonyms and homonyms
· Identifies long vowel sounds by vowel letter
· Recognizes that a single vowel followed by a consonant in a word or syllable has a short vowel sound (there are some exceptions, eg. eat)
· Understands that a single vowel concluding a word or syllable usually is long, eg. me, tiger
· Recognizes that in words containing two vowels, one of which is a final *e*, the final *e* is silent and the other vowel is long, eg. tale
· Recognizes when two vowels are placed next to each other in a word, the first is long and the second is silent, eg. tail (There are many exceptions)
· Realizes that the letter *y* at the end of a word usually is pronounced long *i*, eg. sky

INCIDENTAL/FUNCTIONAL ERRORS

Because of the close network relationship spelling has with receptive, mental integration, and expressive processing, it is difficult to separate primary and secondary errors. These sections will be treated as one general error category under the topics of receptive errors; mental integrational errors and expressive errors.

RECEPTIVE ERRORS

Seeing and hearing deficiencies can contribute to spelling errors, When pronunciation of the word given cannot be perceptually dissected into a letter-sound relationship, a misspelled word will be the result. Similarly, when a word-form cannot be visualized when spelling of that word is requested, an error can be easily made.

When a visual or auditory perceptual difficulty is realized, special effort must be made to present a learning technique that will utilize the receptive skill available to the individual.

MENTAL INTEGRATION ERRORS

Mental integration is directly responsible for any individual being able to master the language arts skill of spelling. The language arts skill of reading is the mental integration process directly influencing accurate word formation. Failures arise when the phonomes and the alphabetic letters are represented differently. Irregularities in English orthography (phonics) are directly related to misspelling. A tendency to transpose, add or omit letters will create immediate spelling irregularities. No systematic method can alter these discrepancies so rote memorization is necessary.

EXPRESSIVE ERRORS

The ability to speak and write cleanly and accurately greatly enhances the coordinating language arts skill of spelling. In speaking, when words are mispronounced or when omissions, substitutions and distortions are made, spelling errors will increase.

Dialect produces speaking language patterns that fail to follow English orthography (phonics). If the person is encouraged to spell as a word sounds then errors are sure to result.

Writing, the written form of a word, may cause spelling errors. Careless use of, or failure to develop good handwriting techniques may cause misperceptions of an accurate word form spelling. Transposing of letters in words is also a common writing problem creating inaccurate spelling.

Spelling Agencies

Better Education through Simplified Spelling
2340 E. Hammond Lake Drive
Bloomfield Hills, MI 48013

American Literary Council (Spelling Emphasis)
106 Morningside Drive
New York, NY 10027

Association for the Encouragement of Correct Punctuation, Spelling, and Usage in Public Communication
88 Garfield Avenue
Madison, NJ 07940

RELATED SERVICES

The All Handicapped Children's Act (AHCA) defines related services as "such developmental, corrective, and other supportive services . . . as may be required to assist a handicapped child to benefit from special education. Related services eligibility is based on the law that a child must be "handicapped" and special education is required. A "related service" must be necessary for a child to benefit from special education. A district's responsibility according to the Act was designed to maintain a "basic floor of opportunity." This floor consists of "access to specialized instruction and related services which are individually designed to provide educational benefit to the handicapped child."

Transportation

Transportation is included as a related service under Education of the Handicapped 20 U.S.C. 1404-1461. It is a part of a "free appropriate public education" assurance component stating that transportation must be provided at public expense, under public supervision and direction, and without charge. Its major purpose is to enable a child to be physically present in class.

Transportation must be provided if the district provides transportation for its general school population. Any school district which provides any special education program must provide transportation to any handicapped person qualifying for the particular special education institution or related service. When a school district does not provide transportation to its general school population it must decide on an individual basis where the transportation benefits the special education of the handicapped individual.

Transportation includes service starting at the vehicle and to the special education and/or related service site or center. It may include to and from residential placement as well. Sites for the visually impaired and hearing impaired where services are found at state facilities, such as the School for the Blind and the School for the Deaf, require of the local school systems a transportation provision. Similar procedures are followed for intersensory handicaps such as the deaf/blind facilities which are geographically difficult to find.

Counseling/Psychological Services

A major component of related services involves both psychological and counseling assistance to handicapped individuals in special education. Public Law 94-142 defines psychological services as including:

"(I) Administering psychological and educational tests and other assessment procedures: (Native tongue required).

(II) Interpreting assessment results:

(III) Obtaining, integrating, and interpreting information about child behavior and conditions relating to learning:

(IV) Consulting with other staff members in planning school programs to meet the special needs of children as indicated by psychological tests, interviews, and behavioral evaluations: and

(V) Planning and managing a program of psychological services, including psychological counseling for children and parents."

Social Work Services in the schools is defined in Public Law 94-142 as including:

"(I) Preparing a social or development history on a handicapped child

(II) Group and individual counseling with the child and family

(III) Working with those problems in a child's living situation (home, school, and community) that affect the child's adjustment in school; and

(IV) Mobilizing school and community resources to enable the child to receive maximum benefit from his or her educational program."

Guidance services are a part of the general education program that participates in the development of an educational plan for each handicapped individual requiring special education related services. The guidance counsellor is frequently the first person to make contact and is in a position to provide continual contact and services. Follow through of individual educational planning and monitoring that progress is often times the responsibility of the counselor.

SOURCES OF PROFESSIONAL HELP

Psychiatrist - A medical doctor specializing in psychiatry or applied behavior disorders.

Psychoanalyst - A medical doctor specializing in a particular field of psychiatry called psychotherapy under the influence of Freud.

Social Worker - Assesses social conditions, interviewing, assists rehabilitation into the community

Neurologist - Focuses on disorders of the nervous system that may influence behavior patterns.

Clinical Psychologist - Performs individual and group therapy sessions, assesses and diagnoses through formal testing procedures—both mental and emotional.

Guidance Counselor - Resides in an educational school site, usually in one building, assisting students who need guidance and counseling in that professional setting.

School Psychologist - Administers and interprets individual psychological and educational tests for gaining information pertinent to an individual educational plan.

Psychometrist - A trained professional in the administration and interpretation of academic achievement and behavioral tests.

Centers for Counseling/ Psychological Evaluation

Child guidance centers - A specialized center staffed with a cluster of trained professionals whose expertise centers around the needs of children.

Hospital psychiatric unit - Specialized areas in general hospital setting designated for intense psychological and counseling services.

Local mental health center - Public facility serving a certain community or designated area and providing services in counseling and psychological assistance. (Cost of services is pro-rated to the economy).

Play therapy - Used with children below the ages of eight, allowing through play to demonstrate how they feel about themselves and who is important in their lives at any designated center.

Group therapy - Interaction within a selected group of individuals to open up and expand communication; used in a designated counseling/psychological center.

Private hospitals - A private setting often centered around a particular philosophy used in treating individuals needing special care.

Psychotherapy - A process or treatment covering various kinds of counseling and guidance, individual, group, child, and family therapy and psychoanalysis.

Psychology - An educational approach studying human behavior using psychological and counseling techniques and procedures.

Medical/Health Services

Medical and health services are for diagnosis and evaluation purposes which help decide whether movement from regular educational programming to special education is essential. Before a child can enter special education a free physical examination from a medical doctor is required. Regulations require "related services" provisions including "school health services." School health services are provided by a qualified school nurse or other designated, qualified person. The service described in the law and its regulations must be reasonable to provide and pertinent to the educational process.

Health information compiled for each child referred to the ARC (Admissions and Release Committee) should contain a written description of medical, physical or pharmacological information which may affect educational performance. The following information may be found in such a report: motor functioning; medication used or on currently; a history of illness and accidents; need for medical assistance; medical limitations; chronic illness; history of drug and alcohol abuse; results of vision and hearing screening; trauma; emotional problems; and previous medical evaluations; services; and hospitalization.

MEDICAL/HEALTH PERSONNEL
School Nurse

The Rules of Special Education 12.17 (1) require a health history as part of the comprehensive evaluation. Professional judgement regarding expanded health evaluations or reports related to potential or identified health problems is a major responsibility. When no health problem is present, a written report is filed into the child's folder. Attendance at individual educational program meetings is expected or information from such meetings should be given in written form to the school nurse. These are the major responsibilities of the school nurse as they relate to special education. The school nurse should assist the handicapped child by providing health care; assist the parents of handicapped children by acting as a liaison regarding health resource sites such as school, home, community; function as a health consultant and resource for school personnel.

Physical Therapist

The physical therapist organizes, develops, and implements a therapy program to minimize the effect of a physical disability or handicapping condition. The specific responsibilities of the physical therapist include: developing gross motor skill development; develop mobility (walking, crawling, wheelchair use, prosthetic devices); recommend equipment and training in the use of adaptive equipment (special chairs, leg braces, positioning equipment); consulting with and training staff in handling/positioning/safety of movements; development and monitoring respiratory functioning programs.

Occupational Therapist

The occupational therapist's role is to minimize the effect of a physical disability or handicapping condition by organizing, developing, and implementing a therapy program of an individual nature. The major roles and responsibilities of the occupational therapist include: a development of fine motor coordination; recommending equipment/training for a student to use in the classroom, for the individual himself, or his/her hand skills (dressing aids, eating aids, special chairs, prosthetic devices, splints); development of sensorimotor skills/sensory integration to classroom performances (motor planning, bilateral integration, tactile defensiveness); develop work simplifications and motor techniques for practical school usage.

School health services are varied from state to state and school district to school district. Many school districts provide little or no assistance in this area because of financial reasons. Health services remain a vital contributor to the special education program in the area of medical and physical facets of the total school program.

MENTAL INTEGRATION DISORDERS

When mental integration problems arising from mental subnormal functioning and irregular mental integration patterns exist, health information is an important related service. Many special education individuals who exhibit problems relating to the brain and its functioning have multi-handicap (multiple type of special problems—sensory, motor) conditions. Health records and health histories are gathered to better facilitate medical and health services.

Health Information

Special emphasis is placed on maintaining current health history which is the responsibility of the school nurse. A cumulative school health record is kept by the school and includes general information (name, address, parent, physician, emergency person's name with address/phone numbers). Primary immunizations and booster immunizations are kept in the record. The history, health conditions, and recommendations section deals with an auxiliary set of conditions found in the child, such as allergies, diabetes, headaches, rubella, stomach disorders, etc. A special space is allowed for medications which list date, drug, and dose. The school nurse keeps a health record of all children and each mental subnormal or malfunctioning individual has such a report in their individual education plan (IEP).

AGENCY DIRECTORY

Information about a particular handicapping condition is often times not generally available. Parents, educators, health professionals, and everyone else who works with a particular identifiable handicap needs additional information about the handicap, services that are necessary and available, and the location of specified services. National organizations on specific disabilities or conditions focuses on information and support. Parent training and parent support groups offer general information, assistance, and support. Government agencies give information relating to laws and services. When help is needed there are many sources available to the handicapped person. When educational practices and general information appear sketchy and vague, help may be found through knowledgeable centers. These centers may be able to clarify the opportunities available to the handicapped person and a clearer route for the person directly involved with that individual who is handicapped.

Agency listings are given with addresses and telephone numbers when possible. Telephone numbers can, however, be obtained by dialing information in the city where the location is found. Do not give up if addresses are incorrect. Interagency information is available at any government center or clearing house. They are generally courteous and will assist the person when a need has been voiced to them.

The list of agencies used is largely found in a fact sheet distributed by NICHCY–The National Information Center for Children and Youth with Disabilities, P.O. Box 1492, Washington, D.C. 20013.

GOVERNMENT AGENCIES
Interprofessional Information

Administration for Children, Youth and Families
P.O. Box 1182
Washington, D.C. 20013
(202) 245-0347

Administration on Developmental Disabilities (DHHS)
329 D Humphrey Building
200 Independence Ave., S.W.
Washington, D.C. 20201
(202) 245-2890

Bureau of Maternal and Child Health and Resources Development
Parklawn Building
5600 Fishers Lane
Rockville, MD 20857
(301) 443-2170

District Internal Revenue Service - Tax Information
(800) 424-1040
(800) 424-FORM

National Institute of Neurological & Communicative Disorders
NIH, Bldg. 31, Room 8A-06
Bethesda, MD 20892
(301) 496-4000

National Library Service for the Blind and Physically Handicapped
Library of Congress
1291 Taylor Street, N.W.
Washington, D.C. 20542
(800) 424-8567

Office of Disease Prevention and Health Promotion
National Health Information Center
P.O. Box 1133
Washington, D.C.
20013-1133, (800) 336-4797

Department of Health and Human Services
(Medicare Information and Second Surgical Opinion Program)
Health Care Financing Administration
Baltimore, MD 21235

National Center for Education in Maternal and Child Health
38th and R Streets, N.W.
Washington, D.C. 20625-8400

National Information Center for Children & Youth with Handicaps (NICHCY)
P.O. Box 1492
Washington, D.C. 20013
(800) 999-5599
(703) 893-6061
(703) 893-8614 (TDD)

National Institute of Child Health and Human Development
NIH, 9000 Rockville Pike
Bldg. 31, Room 2A03
Bethesda, MD 20892
(301) 496-3454

President's Committee on Employment of People with Disabilities
1111 20th St., N.W., Suite 636
Washington, D.C. 20036-3470
(202) 653-5044
(202) 653-5050 (TDD)

Public Information Office
National Library of Medicine
Bethesda, MD 20894
(301) 496-4000

Senate Subcommittee on
Disability Policy
113 Hart Senate Office Bldg.
Washington, D.C. 20510
(202) 224-6265

Social Security Administration Hotline
(800) 234-5SSA
(800) 324-0778 (TDD)
(800) 392-0812 (in Mo./TDD)

Office of Special Education
and Rehabilitation Services
Clearinghouse on Disability Information
U.S. Dept. of Education
Room 3132, Switzer Bldg.,
330 C St., S.W.
Washington, D.C. 20202-2524
(202) 732-1723, (202) 732-1245

Volunteers in Service to America
Foster Grandparent Program
ACTION
Public Affairs Division
1100 Vermont Ave., N.W.
Washington, D.C. 20525

GENERAL INFORMATION

Public Agencies

STATE EDUCATION DEPARTMENT

The State Department staff can answer questions about special education and related services in your state. Many states have special manuals explaining the steps to take. Check to see if one is available. State Department officials are responsible for special education and related services programs in their state for preschool, elementary, and secondary age children.

STATE VOCATIONAL REHABILITATION AGENCY

The state vocational rehabilitation agency provides medical, therapeutics, counseling, education, training, and other services needed to prepare people with disabilities for work. This state agency will provide you with the address of the nearest rehabilitation office where you can discuss issues of eligibility and services with a counselor. The state vocational rehabilitation agency can also refer you to an independent living

program in your state. Independent living programs provide services which enable adults with disabilities to live productively as members of their communities. The services might include, but are not limited to, information and referral, peer counseling, workshops, attendant care, and technical assistance.

OFFICE OF STATE COORDINATOR OF VOCATIONAL EDUCATION FOR HANDICAPPED STUDENTS

States receiving federal funds used for vocational education must assure that funding is used in programs which include students with handicaps. This office can tell you how your state funds are being used and provide you with information on current programs.

STATE MENTAL RETARDATION/DEVELOPMENTAL DISABILITIES AGENCIES

The functions of state mental retardation/developmental disabilities agencies vary from state to state. The general purpose of this office is to plan, administer and develop standards for state/local mental retardation/developmental disabilities programs provided in state-operated facilities and community-based programs. This office provides information about available services to families, consumers, educators and professionals.

STATE DEVELOPMENTAL DISABILITIES COUNCIL

Assisted by the U.S. Department of Health and Human Services' Administration on Developmental Disabilities, state councils plan and advocate for improvement in services for people with developmental disabilities. In addition, funding is made available for time-limited demonstration and stimulatory grant projects.

STATE MENTAL HEALTH AGENCIES

The functions of state mental health agencies vary from state to state. The general purposes of these offices are to plan, administer, and develop standards for state and local mental health programs such as state hospitals and community health centers. They can provide information to the consumer about mental illness and a resource list of contacts where you can go for help.

PROTECTION AND ADVOCACY AGENCY AND CLIENT ASSISTANCE PROGRAM

Protection and advocacy systems are responsible for pursuing legal, administrative and other remedies to protect the rights of people who are developmentally disabled or mentally ill, regardless of their age. Protection and advocacy agencies may provide information about health, residential, and social service in your are. Legal assistance is also available.

The Client Assistance Program provides assistance to individuals seeking and receiving vocational rehabilitation services. These services, provided under the Rehabilitation Act of 1973, include assisting in the pursuit of legal, administrative, and other appropriate remedies to ensure the protection of the rights of individuals with developmental disabilities.

PROGRAMS FOR CHILDREN WITH SPECIAL HEALTH CARE NEEDS

The U.S. Department of Health and Human Services' Office of Maternal and Child Health and Resource Development provides grants to states for direct medical and related services to children with handicapping conditions. Although services will vary from state to state, additional programs may be funded for retraining, research, special projects, genetic disease testing, and counseling services. For additional information about current grants and programs in your state, contact:

National Center for Education in Maternal and Child Health
38th and R Streets, NW
Washington, D.C. 20057.

UNIVERSITY AFFILIATED PROGRAMS

A national network of programs affiliated with universities and teaching hospitals, UAPs provides interdisciplinary training for professionals and paraprofessionals and offers programs and services for children with disabilities and their families. Some UAPs provide direct services for children and families. Individual UAPs have staff with expertise in a variety of areas and can provide information, technical assistance, and inservice training to agencies, service providers, parent groups, and others.

A listing of all University Affiliated Programs may be obtained by contacting:

The Maternal and Child Health Clearing House
38th and R Streets, N.W.
Washington, D.C. 20057.

DISABILITY AGENCIES

Birth Defects

Association of Birth Defect Children
Orlando Executive Park
5400 Diplomat Circle, Suite 270
Orlando, FL 32810

National Birth Defects Center
Franciscan Children's Hospital
30 Warren Street
Boston, MA 02135

March of Dimes Birth Defects Foundation
1275 Mamaroneck Avenue
White Plains, NY 10605

National Network to Prevent Birth Defects
P.O. Box 15309, South East Station
Washington, D.C. 20003

Chromosome 18

Chromosome 18 Society
c/o Jannine Cody
6302 Fox Head
San Antonio, TX 78247

Fragile X Syndrome

National Fragile X Foundation
1441 York Street
Suite 215
Denver, CO 80206

Down's Syndrome

Association for Children with Downs Syndrome
2616 Martin Avenue
Bellmore, NY 11710

Dyslexia

Dyslexia Research Institute, Inc.
4745 Centerville Road
Tallahassee, FL 32308

Huntington's Disease

**Huntington's Disease
Society of America**
140 W. 22nd Street, 5th Floor
New York, NY 10011-2420

Hydrocephalus

National Hydrocephalus Foundation
22427 S. River Road
Joliet, IL 60436

Maple Syrup Urine Disease

**Maple Syrup Urine Disease
Family Support Group**
c/o Bonnie Koons
1045 Piketown Road
Harrisburg, PA 17112

Genetic Conditions

Alliance of Genetic Support Groups
1001 22nd Street, N.W.
Suite 800
Washington, D.C. 20037

Learning Disabilities

**Association for Children and Adults
with Learning Disabilities**
4156 Library Road
Pittsburgh, PA 15234

Marfan Syndrome

National Marfan Foundation
382 Main Street
Port Washington, NY 11050

Trisomy 18, 13

Support Organization for Trisomy 18, 13
c/o Barb Van Herreweghe
2982 So. Union Street
Rochester, NY 14624

**American Printing House
for the Blind**
1839 Frankfort Avenue
P.O. Box 6085
Louisville, KY 40206

Mental Retardation

**Association for Retarded
Citizens of the U.S.**
2501 Avenue J
Arlington, TX 76006

Turner's Syndrome

Turner's Syndrome Society
Administrative Studies Bldg.
Room 006
4700 Keele Street
York University
Downsview, Ontario, Canada M3J 1P3

Vestibular Disorders

Vestibular Disorders Association
1015 N.W. 22nd Avenue
Portland, OR 97210-3079

Mental Integration Processing

**American Association of University
Affiliated Programs for Persons with
Developmental Disabilities (AAUAP)**
8605 Cameron Street, Suite 406
Silver Spring, MD 20910

CHAPTER 4

Manifestation #3 – Expressive Processing

PHYSICAL BODY STRUCTURAL SYSTEMS

COMMUNICATION SKILLS

Communication is the interchange of information or thought by speech, print, signs, or signals for the purpose of sending a message. The major components include utilization of knowledge and skills, interaction among other individuals, and the development of knowledge about the world around them. The speech parts involved in communication include voice (quality, pitch, loudness, resonance), articulation, and fluency.
The language communication components include form of language, content of language, and language functioning.

STRUCTURAL/SKELETAL SYSTEMS

The ability to help the structural capacity of an individual to maintain a straight and normal condition is the responsibility of the skeletal or structural system. It is sometimes labeled the orthopedic system. Body involvement includes the use of nerves, muscles, or bones for the purpose of physical mobility. Legs, arms, joints, and the spine are the key body parts that are involved.

HEALTH RELATED SYSTEMS

The health related system includes those components designed to achieve a set of purposes to attain a standard degree of health within a given human being. These systems generally influence strength, vitality, and alertness. Included among such body functions are the metabolism, lungs, heart, blood, nervous system, and basic cell production.

**Physical Structure for All Individuals
Suffering with Handicapping Characteristics**

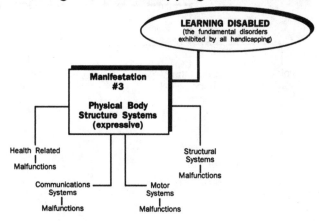

MOTOR SYSTEM

Motor skills are requiring the ability to control and direct the voluntary muscles of the body. They are generally classified as gross motor activity and fine motor activity. Gross motor activity involves movement in which groups of large muscles are employed for balance and rhythm. Fine motor skills involve the output of the delicate muscle system. The motor learning developmental skills involved include:
(a) basic input system such as reflexes, vestibular, etc.;
(b) basic abilities involving the perceptual motor system, physical fitness and motor fitness;
(c) basic expressive skills involving walking, stair-climbing, and functional skills (locomotion).

COMMUNICATION SYSTEMS

Definition by P.L. 94-142

The definition for individuals receiving federal assistance under the law is:

"Communication disorders such as stuttering, impaired articulation, a language impairment, or a voice impairment, which adversely affects a child's educational performance."

This definition is general by nature and encompasses a broad selection of problems that may produce a speech or language disorder.

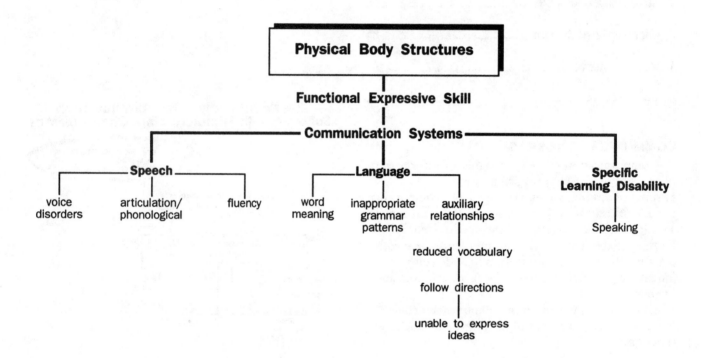

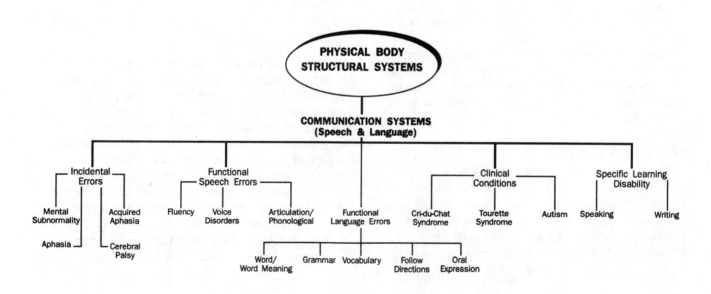

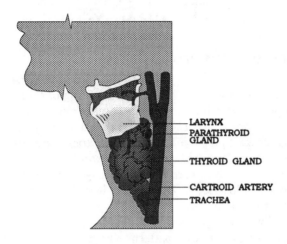

LARYNX
PARATHYROID GLAND
THYROID GLAND
CARTROID ARTERY
TRACHEA

Speech/Language Terminology

ADDITION
An improper addition of phonemes of words rather than a faulty production of a phoneme.

APHASIA
A brain injury where there is an interference with the comprehension and use of language.

APHONIA
An organic psychic inability to speak.

ARTICULATION
The production of sounds of speech in a sequential or continuous developmental series.

AUTISM
A developmental disorder involving social interaction and communication which may result in deviant behavior patterns.

DISTORTION
An approximated production of a phoneme which is unacceptable articulation.

DYSARTHRIA
An inability to intelligently articulate speech sounds of cerebral origin producing incoordination, paralysis, and/or weakness in the speech mechanism.

FLUENCY
The speech-flow of language involving the smooth flow of sounds, syllables, words, and phrases as they are joined together.

LANGUAGE
An established system of communication using linguistic symbols to convey meaning to human beings.

LINGUISTICS
A scholarly study of the function and nature of language.

MORPHEME
A combination of phonemes that produce meaningful combinations of sounds from which words are built.

OMISSION
The absence of appropriate phonemes resulting in an inaccurate articulation of a word.

PHONEME
The smallest unit of sound capable of producing variations which change meanings.

PHONOLOGY
A linguistic system of communication involving the study of word formation and deviation (word unit meanings).

SEMANTICS
A linguistic study of word changes and their meanings.

SPEECH
An established system of oral communication beginning with the birth cry and developmental through maturational stages.

SUBSTITUTION
A substitution of inaccurate phonemes for an otherwise normal phoneme.

SYNTACTIC ORDER
An arrangement of words (morphemes) in a meaningful order to relate one idea to another.

SYNTAX
A linguistic system of language involving arrangement and order of words (grammar).

Checklists

Speech Checklist

Misarticulaton
· Omission of phoneme
· Substitution of phoneme
· Distortion of phoneme
· Addition of phoneme

Voice Problems
· Pitch
    · Highness/lowness
    · Shrill
    · Unusual pitch (age/sex)
· Intensity
    · Too loud
    · Uncontrollable loudness
    · Too soft
    · Voicelessness
· Quality
    · Nasal voice
    · Breathy
    · Hoarse
    · Harsh
· Flexibility
    · Monotone
    · Mumbling
    · Indistinct phonemes

Rhythm/fluency
- Sequence/order of phoneme
- Mispronunciation/length of time of phoneme
- Speaking/rate of phoneme occurrence
- Rhythm/pattern of phoneme occurrence
- Smoothness of phoneme occurrence

Language Checklist

Words and their meanings
- Difficulty in recognizing letters
- Difficulty in recognizing words
- Difficulty in recognizing a symbol (Subject oriented)
- Difficulty in recognizing graphic symbols
- Difficulty in map skills

Reduced Vocabulary
- Inability to store sound patterns
- Inability to recall word patterns
- Inability to recall word meanings
- Inability to recall sentence structure
- Inability to recall concepts

Inappropriate grammar patterns
- Inability to produce a sound(s) (phoneme)
- Inability to produce a word(s) (morpheme)
- Inability to formulate sentence structure (syntax)

Inability to follow directions
- Pay attention
- Make choices
- Respond to questions
- Develop limits in behavior
- Participate in group activity
- Attempt a new skill
- Make a selection

Inability to express ideas
- Limited vocabulary
- Poor sentence structure
- Inability to complete a sentence
- Inability to name an object
- Inability to categorize an object
- Inability to describe an object
- Inability to report on an action
- Inability to report on what he/she is doing

SPEECH AND LANGUAGE STRUCTURAL SYSTEMS

COMMUNICATION SYSTEMS

Communication is the ability to express ideas and wants into words so that understanding of those words and concepts have meaning. The three major functions for this to occur involve speech, hearing, and language. Speech and language are tools used for communication. Hearing is a receptive sensory stimulus that leads to speech and language. Because hearing is a receptive sensory process, it is included in that section. Definitions included:

Speech: A way of using breath in the production of sounds in precise patterns which produces understandable words.

Language: A communication system linking hearing and speech. It functions through spoken and written symbols representing conventional meaning.

INCIDENTAL ERRORS

MENTAL SUBNORMALITY

Speech and language problems may manifest themselves through functional mental subnormality. Language is an especially important concept in the measurement of intelligence on an individual I.Q. test. Children who lack the cultural background and language experiences tend to score lower. When these factors are persistently developmentally deficient in the growth of speech and language skills the individuals scores may fall into the mental subnormality range. When a child's I.Q. score falls below 75 he/she may be classified as mentally subnormal and be placed in a setting with these children and this type of educational programming. It is extremely important when evaluation is taking place with both oral and written words that proper consideration be given to diagnostic evaluation including those tests relating solely to speech and language communication rather than having general intelligence testing being the basic source of evaluation.

Language learning which may influence such a difficulty may be expressive or receptive by nature. Expressive language may fail to develop but comprehension will be intact. Receptive deficiencies may be the result of failure for expressive and/or receptive language mechanisms to develop at a normal pace. Age-appropriate concepts may also inhibit growth of normal language measurement. Failure in understanding and use of common objects may result in developmental delays. It is important to remember that mental subnormality is directly related to language competencies and should be considered only as functioning characteristics of individuals who are predominantly having speech and language (communication) problems.

Assistance is available through speech and language specialists who can make interpretations where primary speech and language disorders are concerned. Two major areas of concern should include the formation and development of appropriate speech (sounds) and the formation of the word(s) and its social and communicative relationship in society (language). The ability to acquire and learn meaningful language patterns may offset an inappropriate behavior called mental subnormality.

CEREBRAL PALSIED

Cerebral palsy results in a muscular weakness or paralysis. Articulation problems and speech selection and sequences are directly affected. Muscles which control breathing, formation of sound units (phonation), sound quality (resonation), and articulate physical movement are major contributing factors to faulty speech problems. The cerebral palsied victim's brain injury may also include a language disorder as well. Perception and mental integrational functioning may cause irregular language and communication problems. Speech and language specialists must consider special plans and plan appropriate strategies for possible remediation. Because muscle injury and/or deterioration may result, progress in correction may be little or even impossible. However, established remedial techniques and methods are available and should be attempted to aid in the total communication system of the victim of cerebral palsy.

CLEFT LIP AND PALATE

Abnormalities of the mouth and face frequently interfere with the normal development of speech. The cleft lip and/or palate defect occurs during the eighth week of pregnancy when the mouth and palate are being formed. The speech mechanism that formulates accurate and appropriate oral language is affected physically, including the tongue, lip, nasal passages, ear, teeth, gums, and palate.

Defective speech communication is the direct result of such a problem. Special assistance from specialists relating to formation and production of speech itself is essential. Because corrective surgery is able to successfully repair this defect on any given infant or young child, articulation corrective techniques should be effective in restoring accurate speech.

ACQUIRED APHASIA

A developmental language disorder which interferes with the comprehension and use of language is acquired aphasia (American Heart Association). It is a condition that results from an injury to the brain following an illness or accident. Strokes are one of the major causes of aphasia.

The problem of speech and language in the aphasia victim varies depending on the location of the injury within the brain itself. Generally both the production and understanding of speech is affected. Speech production involvement includes the lack of motor control and the inability to imitate voice mechanisms relating to the jaw, lip, and tongue. Mental capacity may also affect and contribute to these speech irregularities.

Understanding of speech may be the direct result of receptive/sensory processing. Muteness, scribble speech, echolalia, and phase choice may symbolically show that inability to appropriate accurate perceptual speech patterns for communicating with individuals or in social situations. Difficulty in reading and writing may also be observed.

Aphasics may need assistance in producing a normal speech flow. Fluency problems associated with the aphasic include disruptions in voice quality, volume, and inflections. Nonverbal communication is often affected due to the inability of the victim to use gestures.

SPEECH

FUNCTIONAL ERRORS

VOICE DISORDERS

Voice disorders are the result of a malfunctioning of the vocal mechanism. The sound generating system (larynx and vocal chords) produce the vibrations necessary for speech. Air pressure is furnished by the lungs, windpipe, and chest cavity and set the chords vibrate. The throat and oral and nasal passages (resonating system) regulate the wave patterns and produce tones called the normal voice. Variations or mechanical irregularities may produce deviant voice patterns. These speaking voice deviancies are classified as problems in pitch, intensity (loudness), and quality.

Pitch

The highness or lowness of speech may not be in harmony with a person's age or sex. This may produce social and personal problems. Unusual voice patterns are annoying to the listener. Pitch patterns are considered as male, female, or child. Deviations from these patterns are classified as a voice disorder.

Intensity

The loudness and softness of the voice may become unpleasant to the listener. Intensity of speech is monitored by the social situation at hand. Excessive loudness may be cause for reprimanding although it is often the primary characteristic of a hearing impaired child. The "shy" voice is often considered the voice of an unsure individual. Temporary loss of voice may be the consequence of a severe emotional or personal problem. Psychiatric assistance may be sought instead of aid from a speech communications expert.

Quality

The most frequent voice disorder is voice quality. When vocal characteristics become odd and distracting, help is suggested. A problem centering in the resonating system (throat and oral and nasal passage) can produce voice features of huskiness, hoarseness, harshness (strident), and breathy voice quality. Definitions are as follows:

BREATHY VOICE QUALITY - The vocal chords are not brought closely together enough during sound production, thus producing a "whisper effect."

NASAL VOICE QUALITY - The resonance system of the vocal system is malfunctioning, causing a "nasal effect."

HOARSE VOICE QUALITY - An inflammation of the larynx and vocal folds produces this voice variation.

HARSH VOICE QUALITY - Muscular tension in the throat and larynx produces a strained effect on the voice. Strident is the term for the harsh tone of the high pitch.

ARTICULATION DISORDERS

Articulation is the ability to produce the sounds of speech. An articulation disorder involves the inability to produce accurate sounds (phonemes) which involve word productions. There are three major causes for an individual to have faulty articulation. They are:

1. **Organic conditions** - mispronunciation may result from a physical or organic problem, such as impaired hearing, cleft palate, or cerebral palsy. The teeth, hard palate (roof of mouth), and tongue are key articulatory structures which produce a phoneme (consonant or vowel sound). Any such physical deformity that appears results in a poor production of a given word.

2. **Faulty Learning** - A failure to learn the correct patterns of normal speech. Faulty speech patterns may arise from poor speech models or lack of stimulation or motivation to produce a word accurately.

3. **Emotional adjustment** - Involves the adverse conditions in the environment that surround the child which may result in misarticulation to complete absence of or refusal to use speech. This may

be classified as withdrawing from unpleasant situations in the immediate environment. Withdrawal symptoms are considered under the section Seriously Emotionally Disturbed.

Actual errors in the accurate production of a word take on the form of a sound being substituted, omitted, or distorted. This makes the speaker difficult to understand. The young child makes many such errors when learning to produce sounds and words. When their speech calls attention to itself or is unintelligible, special services should be considered.

OMISSIONS

An omission is an inappropriate absence of a particular sound. This irregular speech pattern is frequently found when a final consonant is omitted in the production of a word (meat/mi). Whole syllables may also be omitted from a word. When two consonants formulate a blend sound (st, bl, etc.), one of the consonants is often left out. These patterns are regularly found in young children learning sound and word production.

SUBSTITUTION

The production constitutes an unacceptable approximation of a particular speech sound. An individual may produce something that nears actual phoneme or desired word production but causes a distortion of the word itself. The most commonly distorted sound is "s."

FLUENCY (Stuttering & Cluttering)

Melody and rhythm of the spoken word constitutes the fluency of the speaker. At approximately 3 years of age, expressive language becomes a verbal part of the communication process. At this time the child leaves the communication world of jargon (make-believe language) and puts meaningful phrases into complete thought patterns (sentences). It is at this time that irregularities in speech flow (fluency) begin to appear. All speakers exhibit interruptions in their oral communication, but abnormality of speech fluency exists when one listens more to how a person talks rather than to what that person says. Speaking too rapidly, reversing sound order, stumbling, and backtracking, repeating words/syllables, and pausing in the wrong place in the sentence, constitute disturbances in the rhythm and flow of speech (fluency).

The two disorders of fluency include stuttering and cluttering. Stuttering is considered a disorder of speech production that lacks normal fluency. Cluttering is diagnosed as a speech production problem involving indistinct, garbled, and unintelligible production of sounds and words.

STUTTERING

Stuttering is the major fluency problem characterized by repetition of sounds, syllables, and often of entire words or phrases. It may involve abnormal hesitations and prolongations. This fluency problem is accompanied by body movements such as grimaces and gestures. Stuttering is most characteristic for its interruption of speech flow.

Stuttering is a mystery disorder. Usually considered as a major problem in speech and language, its involvement is in only 1% of the general population, making it a minor communication problem. It is consistently found in males over females. Stuttering develops between the ages of 3-9 years. Those afflicted tend to develop speech and language problems at a later age. This fluency problem tends to run in families.

The language and speech pattern that interrupts the flow of oral communication includes:
1. Production of 90% of words is normal leaving 10% where irregular flow pattern is observed.
2. A typical stuttering lasts one to two seconds.
3. Stuttering patterns vary from individual to individual with no two exactly alike.
4. Most individuals report stuttering in certain periods of time in their life.
5. Stutterers tend to have minor problems in language communication, such as when singing or speaking in rhythm.
6. The physical and mechanical movements appear unaffected.
7. Words most likely to create fluency problems include: words beginning with consonants, words beginning a sentence, longer than average words, words occurring as nouns, verbs, adverbs, and adjectives.

Because of the extreme aggravated fluency interruption pattern, stuttering is noted and reacted to by the average listener. Anxieties, fears, and apprehensions often accompany the stutterer, but for what reason is not quite sure.

CLUTTERING

The fluency of speech found by the clutterer includes rapid enunciation which becomes distorted, sounds may be substituted, and words or word parts are omitted. It mainly involves the rate and rhythm of oral communication.

Cluttering and stuttering are considered by many as an overlapping or same fluency problem. Both involve a disruptive pattern in rate and rhythm. Clutterers, however, appear willing to talk at length, whereas stutterers appear to have great anxiety and fear when communicating orally.

Characteristically, it is believed by phonicatrists that a central language imbalance produces this verbal manifestation. Lack of awareness of the problem, short attention span, and excessive repetitions accompany this fluency disorder. Speech itself is demonstrative of excessive rate, garbled speech, and erratic rhythm by the clutterer.

LANGUAGE—STRUCTURAL SYSTEM

Language is a systematic link between hearing and speech. It shapes the social as well as the intellectual aspects of each individual. Receptively, it requires the ability to comprehend and relate the spoken word to the appropriate unit of experience. Language is an expressive tool which provides communication for each person. Useful expressive communication includes speaking, reading, and writing. Socially, it helps shape and convey a person's social being.

Language learning disabilities reflect problems in communication skills involving a person's inability to comprehend, interpret, and express meaning. Developmental language delay involves the following factors: improper use of words and their meaning, inappropriate grammatical patterns, reduced vocabulary, inability to follow directions or to express ideas.

WORD MEANING

The fundamental unit of communication is the ability to perceive, understand, and interpret the basic unit—the word. Vocabulary is the accumulation of words an individual is able to comprehend and use. Acquiring vocabulary is a complex progressive process. It requires the acquisition of the basic phoneme patterns (sounds) as well as the morpheme patterns (words).

Vocabulary acquisition is a cumulative learning process involving both receptive vocabulary acquisition as well as an expressive vocabulary. Developmental stages may follow this pattern.

Receptive Language
0 to 2 years
- hears sound
- cries when hearing crying
- selects sounds
- memorizes sounds
- makes social noise
- responds to outside sounds (dog barking)
- distance sound reaction
- imitates sounds
- answers oral commands

3 to 4 years
- understands 1,000 to 2,000 words
- repeats four-word-long sentences
- understands verbs, adjectives, pronouns, prepositions
- compares speech with others
- understands 90% of what he/she says

5 to 7 years
- comprehends 4,000 words
- comprehends word structure
- understands time intervals

Expressive Language

0 to 2 years
- discomfort sounds
- comfort sounds (vowel, consonant)
- babble
- vocal play
- inflections
- first words
- vocalization (jargon, echolalia)
- compound words
- simple/compound sentences

3 to 4 years
- speaking vocabulary (900-1,000 words)
- uses different word forms
- knows sizes
- controls voice quality
- mastered vowel and diphthong sounds

5 to 7 years
- speaks standard English
- 2,500 word vocabulary
- gives/receives information
- begins abstract thinking
- asks for explanation
- perceives motives of action

INAPPROPRIATE GRAMMATICAL PATTERNS

Grammar lies between the speech sounds you hear or say and the meanings connected with them. It is systematic by mature. Grammar involves the set of rules that generate any and all permissible utterances in that language. Syntax is used to denote the order or arrangement of words. Production may be classified as follows:

1 to 2 years
- communicates relationships by vocal cues
- communicates relationships by body cues
- communicates relationships by changing a topic word

2 to 3 years
- changes word order
- communicates complicated relationships

3 to 7 years
- refines sentence structure
- categorizes different words

5 to 10 years
- varies structures of language to meet expressive communication needs.

Incidental Involvement

LANGUAGE—CLINICAL TYPES

AUTISM

Autism is a developmental disability originating by 3 years of age which interferes with skill development in the area of speech and language, fine motor skill delays, and social-adaptive and cognitive processes. This biologically based disorder affects two-way social interaction and communication. Behavior problems arise or intertwine with communicative problems. Psychological environmental factors have not been shown to cause autism. Arrests, delays, and regression, however, may occur among or within one or more of the pathways.

Sensory stimuli disturbances and inappropriate responses often occur in "autistic-like" children. Symptoms in visual, auditory, tactile, vestibulary, olfactory, and proprioceptive (sensory perceptor positioned within the body) systems are observed. Repetitive movements involve such manifestations as rocking and spinning, head banging, and hand twisting. Activity levels vary from high to low within a given autistic individual. Disturbances related to people, events, and objects manifest themselves with inappropriate or unresponsive behavior. Responses to adults and peers develop but are oftentimes superficial, immature, and only in response to strong social cues. The use of toys and objects is often unconventional, and little imaginative play is observed.

The primary disorder facing the autistic-like child is his/her inability to communicate in regular social situations requiring communication. Speech may be absent or delayed at an early age. Articulation problems prevail with noticeably immature or inappropriate reflexes being produced. The structure of the sentence may be heard while major characteristics may be noticeably immature.

Checklist for Autism

SENSORY PROBLEMS
- hyperactive
- fascinated with trivial details
- staring
- non-use of eye contact
- prolonged look at hand/objects
- unresponsive to sound
- over-responsive to sound
- overreaction to self-induced sounds
- over-responsive to touch
- under-responsive to touch
- over-responsive to pain
- under-responsive to pain
- over-responsive to temperature
- under-responsive to temperature
- prolonged rubbing of a surface
- sensitivity to food texture
- preoccupation with moving objects
- whirls around without dizziness
- licks inedible objects
- sniffs inappropriately
- hand flapping
- grimaces
- gesticulates
- poor patterns of posture

SPEECH/LANGUAGE
- nonlogical use of concepts
- neologisms (new meaning for established words)
- limited symbolic ability
- inability to reason
- inability to conceptualize
- inability to comprehend abstractions
- gestures inappropriately
- gestures unrelated to language
- delayed development of gestures
- inappropriate pitch
- inappropriate pronunciation
- poor volume control
- negative echolalia
- language deficit in play

MOTOR DISTURBANCES
- inability to learn to skip
- inability to learn to dance
- inability to learn to swim
- difficulty in throwing a ball
- confused with left/right
- confused with up/down
- confused with back/front
- reverses letters (b and d)
    - (p and q)
    - (m and w)
- puts clothes on backwards

SOCIAL DISTURBANCES
- keeps same routine
- change produces screams/tantrums
- attached to objects
- lacks imagination in play
- lacks social requirements by
    - -screaming in public
    - -grabbing store items
    - -kicking/biting people
    - -kicking/biting him/herself
- failure to develop cooperative play
- immature/superficial response to adults

SPECIAL SKILLS
- loves music
- sings well
- enjoys jig-saw puzzles
- prefers construction toys
- mechanical by nature
- calculates complicated math concepts
- composes tunes
- plays musical instruments

CRI-DU-CHAT
"Cat's-Cry Syndrome"

The Cri-du-Chat syndrome is characterized by a high pitched, mewing cry, resembling the cry of a kitten which is heard in it's first weeks of newborn life. It disappears but characteristics remaining include low set, malformed ears, microcephaly (small head/skull), and mental retardation. There is high infant mortality rate. If the infant survives, special education services will be needed.

GILES DE LA TOURETTE SYNDROME

A childhood disorder which begins with grunting or barking noises involving respiratory and vocal systems. The progression of the disease may lead to convulsive utterances. The involuntary, obsessive type utterances may become severe enough to be physically and socially disabling. Tourette Syndrome is classified under the medical topic of disorders of movement commonly known as tics. Drug therapy may be introduced to reduce the movement.

REDUCED VOCABULARY, INABILITY TO FOLLOW DIRECTIONS OR EXPRESS IDEAS

Understanding language results in a learned process involving the ability to attend, select, memorize, recall, and match. Children's failure to learn proper communication may results from an inability to attain a working vocabulary, an inability to interpret oral expression by following directions, and an inability to express ideas relating to a given communication.

Possible factors involve include:
- difficulty in oral-motor control (lip, tongue, and jaw movement)
- failure to follow simple commands
- inability to identify common objects by pointing
- inability to arrange objects
- positioning of objects in sequence
- inability to note details
- failure to answer specific questions about an immediate experience

The ultimate goal for communication is the functional use of the skills relating to making the symbol word meaningful. Language becomes an important tool in total communication. The process of learning becomes so interrelated that it is difficult to separate or categorize. Key issues of learning and their involvement with speech and language cannot be covered in this section.

Communication specialists are aware of the language difficulties of any child or adult. Individuals directly involved with language deficiencies may well assist in activities suggested by professionals in this area.

Language development is noticeably delayed. There is an inability to develop abstract terms, and concepts and reasoning are noticeably inept or immature. Creation of normal language patterns is developmentally delayed with arrests, delays, and regressions common. Logical use of language is especially difficult.

Nonverbal communication is absent or delayed developmentally. Gestures are either absent or inappropriate. As in language development, gestures with symbolic meaning are seldom appropriately interpreted or used.

Specific Learning Disability

A disorder in one or more of the basic psychological processes involved in understanding or in using language, spoken or written, which may manifest itself in an imperfect ability to listen, think, speak, read, write, spell, or to do mathematical calculations. The term includes such conditions as perceptual handicaps, brain injuries, minimal brain dysfunction, dyslexia, and developmental aphasia. The term does not include children who have learning problems which are primarily the result of visual, hearing, or motor handicaps, of mental retardation, of emotional disturbance, or of environmental, cultural, or economic disadvantage.

As defined in the regulations from P.L. 94-142)

SPEAKING

DYSPHASIA

Speaking is an expressive educational problem involving the individual's inability to generate and express ideas or concepts orally. When the severity of the problem interferes with normal learning in the educational setting, special concern and attention is given. Dysphasia is the inability to speak or understand words because of a brain lesion.

Speech is dependent upon many body parts functioning cooperatively. The key to speech is listening, and when the ears are failing to function, speaking will be affected. When a conductive hearing loss is diagnosed, the sounds are faint at any frequency measurement. The outer and middle ears are damaged so that sound cannot reach the cochlea in the inner ear. Ear infections and hardened wax of the outer ear cause such a problem. The characteristics of conductive hearing losses include poor pronunciation of words, failure to follow requests and requires extremely loud volumes on TV, radio, and stereo.

Sensory-neural loss is a hearing impairment where nerve cells or nerve pathways of the inner ear fail to function properly. The sounds affected at certain frequency ranges depend upon the nerve cells that are affected. Sensory-neural loss victims can hear but fail to interpret different sound frequencies accurately. Their speech is distorted causing communication with parents and peers to become impossible because of distortion in a particular hearing range. For example, a child may be able to hear vowel sound frequencies but not consonant sound frequencies accurately.

Speech can be distorted when the muscles or the structure of the mouth or vocal tract are malformed. Physical structures involved in producing speech and the muscles required for the maneuvering of these structures are responsible for the malformation of the speech sounds causing the child to be misunderstood. A common misdiagnosis is an emotional problem rather than a speech distortion. A careful physical examination is important for this speech distortion problem.

Many speech problems arise from impaired language functions which center in the mental integration processing. Failure to formulate ideas into words, memory difficulties involving short and long-term recall of sound patterns and words, and attention span deficits deter good speech communication. Normal intelligence is present and there appears to be no neurological damage. Special teaching techniques by specially trained speech professionals are necessary.

The otolaryngologist, audiologist, and speech pathologist are key specialists for information in this field.

VOCABULARY

Fluency: the flow of speech.

Disfluency: any break in the smooth flow of speech.

Stuttering: a quantity or type of disfluency.

Omission: the leaving out of a sound in speaking.

Substitution: says one sound in place of another.

Distortion: a sound incorrectly produced.

Receptive language: the understanding of speech.

Expressive language: communication of needs, thoughts, and ideas by speech.

Otitis media: inflammation in the middle ear, usually associated with fluid buildup, causing hearing loss.

Articulation: Process by which sounds, syllables and words are formed.

Larynx: produces the sound which we call voice.

Pitch: the speaking level of the sound produced by the larynx.

Intensity: loudness or softness of the sound produced by the larynx.

Quality: the sound resonance or nasality of the voice (hoarse, breathy, etc.)

Aphonia: the failure to voice the articulation will cause speech to be whispered or merely mouthed.

Cluttering: An articulation problem involving rate and rhythm.

Dysarthria: inability to control muscles involving speaking.

Dyspraxia: inability to produce sequential, rapid, precise movements.

Dysphasia: inability to speak or understand words because of a brain lesion.

Phonological impairment: term used to describe misarticulation.

Edema: swelling of the chords after voice misuse.

Polyps: small growths found on the vocal cords.

Checklist

· Omits a sound
· Misarticulates a sound
· Duplicates certain sound
· Skips a syllable
· Cannot produce sequential movements
· Cannot produce rapid, precise movements
· Speaks in a slow, halting manner
· Has false starts when beginning speech
· Cannot understand rules of grammar
· Has difficulty with complex sentences
· Inaccurate information
· Limited information
· Has poor voice quality/pitch
· Has poor volume
· Has inflection difficulties
· Disfluency speech patterns
   -sound
   -syllable repetitions
   -word repetitions
   -phrase repetitions
   -prolongations
   -interjections
   -revisions
   -silent pauses
   -silent blocks

Incidental Involvement

A variety of conditions may contribute to the fact a given individual may encounter problems in generating ideas and concepts and expressing them. Mental integration processing, neurological problems, and physical defects may indirectly produce poor speech.

Mental Integration Processing: The generating of ideas and concepts often produces noticeable defective language patterns. Categories included are disorders involving mental subnormal functioning, aphasia, and autism. Autism involvement may also be classified under physical deformities as well because of its unknown diagnostic origin.

Neurological Injuries: Dysphasia is the inability to produce speech because of neurological damage which includes the cerebral palsied and occasionally spina bifida victims.

Physical Deformities: Speech articulation patterns are influenced by properly formed organs and muscles that directly influence the production of sound. Speech production is imitation of an individual in the immediate environment. When a child cannot hear properly or not at all, speech formation becomes difficult. Malocclusions of the mouth, throat, and larynx will distort speech. Cleft palate is one such deficiency. Stuttering and cluttering are disruptive to the fluency of speech, thus producing distorted language patterns in oral communication.

Functional Involvement

VOICE PRODUCTION

Speech is expressive language used to orally communicate thoughts, ideas, and needs. It includes vocabulary, sentence length, and sentence complexity. Voice is the sound produced by the larynx which is located in the neck. Production of voice involves the lungs generating air so that it passes through the vocal chords like a valve, vibrating these chords. The "normal voice" exhibits an appropriate pitch (sex-orientation measurement used), quality (husky, harsh, breathy), and intensity (loudness/softness). Voice is a problem when attention is placed on how the speaker communicates rather than what he says.

Problems in voice are caused by paralysis of a vocal fold. Misuse of the voice by talking or yelling too loudly or speaking in at pitch level which is too high or too low produces hoarseness. Improper breathing patterns may produce an irregular voice pattern. The chords of the larynx can be damaged through excessive smoking.

Conditions that might affect voice production may include swelling of the vocal chords (edema). Misuse of the voice may also cause formation of vocal nodules, nodes, polyps, or contact ulcers.

ARTICULATION PRODUCTION

Articulation is the process by which sounds, syllables, and words are formed when the tongue, jaw teeth, lips, and palate alter the air stream coming from the vocal chords. Articulation problems occur as a unique problem in cleft palate. Cerebral palsy, hearing deficiencies, and dental problems can influence misarticulation.

The three major types of sound errors are omissions, substitutions, and distortions. Examples include:

Omission:	"at" for "hat"
	"oo" for "shoe"
Substitution:	"wabbit" for "rabbit"
	"thun" for "sun"
Distortion:	inaccurate sound

FLUENCY PROBLEMS

Normal speech is a sequence of movements involving timing and patterns of rate called fluency. When there is an involuntary repetition, prolonging, or blocking of a word, or part of a word, or timing and rate are disrupted, this is called disfluency. Disfluencies occur most frequently on first words spoken in phrases and in sentences. Words patterns and sounds are frequently mispronounced and often are associated with a particular person's disfluencies rather than a general word list. The duration of disfluency lasts two seconds or more. Disfluency origins may vary from where the larynx or voice production are, to where struggles and tensions are observed, to the physical movements of the jaws, tongue, etc. Disfluency problems are very individual in nature.

Dysfluency patterns are generally observed at an early age (2 years). They indicate a struggle with movements producing sounds/eventually words, sentences. It is not a disease or caused by a disease.

Speech Agencies

Speech Communications Association
5105 Bachlick Road, Bldg. F
Annandale, VA 22003

Cured Speech Center
P.O. Box 31345
Raleigh, NC 27622

Foundation for Fluency
9242 Gross Point Road #305
Skokie, IL 60077

International Foundation for Stutterers
P.O. Box 462
Belle Mead, NJ 08502

National Center for Stuttering
200 E 33rd Street
New York, NY 10016

Specific Learning Disability

WRITING

EXPRESSIVE

Writing has the major functions of being a tool for communication as well as being a form of art. As an instrument of practical communication, its purpose is to reveal, record, and clarify experiences. This revelation of self through ideas expressed through the written word, both emotional and intellectual by nature, creates an artistic function.

Writing is more limiting than oral communication. The mechanical conventions of English are involved in creating limitations in legibility and correctness of form. Mechanical elements in punctuation, spelling, and handwriting are controls that regulate and sometimes limit the writing process of the individual having specific learning difficulties. Objectives of the writing program are, however, precise and easy to follow successfully.

VOCABULARY

Written language
ability to write sentences and paragraphs that are understandable and structurally accurate.

Syntax
transmission of the ideas into written words which follows accurate composition and structured patterning.

Orthography
the phonetic approach to understanding sound better, sound-syllable and sound-word relationship.

Lexicology
variations found in orthographic study of sound-word relationships creating spelling variations.

Semantics
the relationship between word meanings and context.

Structure
the mechanical aspects of written expression involving capitalization, punctuation, and rules of grammar.

Paragraph
the fundamental structure of written communication.

Spelling
the coordination of the language arts which promotes accurate information to the reader.

Writing style
the written choice of written format to convey effective communication on paper to the reader.

Format
the organization of thoughts and ideas used to present written communication.

Creativity
the art of writing with self-portraiture thoughts and feelings.

Self-expression
communication involving satisfied presentation of thoughts, feelings, and experiences.

Checklist

· Ability to form letters/words legibly.
· Ability to write a correct sentence.
· Ability to write a paragraph with accuracy.
· Know appropriate punctuation skills.
· Know appropriate capitalization skills.
· Can outline a given passage.
· Can generate a topic idea.
· Has an illustrative vocabulary.
    -adjective
    -verbs
    -pronouns
    -adverbs
    -nouns
    -prepositions
    -conjunctions
· Can tell a joke.
· Can tell a story orally.
· Can spell accurately.
· Has a formal knowledge of the use of a dictionary.
· Can find information in an encyclopedia.
· Has a variety of experiences.
· Recognizes story elements.
    -setting
    -conflict
    -resolution

Incidental Involvement

LANGUAGE PROBLEMS

Language problems are instrumental in interfering with good written expression. Language is communication of social membership. It has its own universal characteristics. Language has its own system which is generally complex evolving around the environment of the person expressing written ideas through their self-developed vocabulary.

Problems arise when language development fails to develop the unusual characteristics required for written communication. When the language system involving sound-letter association, structural composites of the paragraph (word, sentence, tense), have failed to develop, the written composition is effected.

The meaning, form, and functions of language make for a very complex learning process. Failure to perform accurately and intelligently cause breakdown in written communication. Aphasia and autism are examples of such failures.

HEARING PROBLEMS

Written communication is based on the knowledge of sound-word (phoneme-grapheme) correspondence. Oral language competencies make written expression effective. Failure to hear these relationships leads to difficulties in composition and structure of the written word. Spelling patterns are influenced as well. Adjustment may need to be made in instructional planning before written communication, both as a tool and an art, can be effective.

Functional Involvement

Writing for Communication:

The basic objectives of writing require the handicapped individual to have the following tools to make written communication successful. They include the competency of composition, vocabulary selection, syntax-transmissionary meaning, and spelling-lexical word representation found in the English orthography.

COMPOSITION

In writing, the paragraph is the central unit of composition. For paragraph effectiveness, a command of structure, knowledge of the unit of a sentence and grammar element (tense, parts of speech, punctuation, capitalization), is essential. Outlines of the desired written product promote an intellectual and logical format in paragraph sequence.

VOCABULARY SELECTION

Written communication should include the familiar vocabulary which promotes accuracy in spelling. New and exciting words help in present new information. It helps to focus on the ideas they wish to convey. Writing vocabulary selection should encourage new words and recently obtained information. Encouragement of broadening vocabulary and information can increase the learning experiences of the specific learning disabled child.

SYNTAX – TRANSMISSION OF MEANING

The organization of information in a sentence structure should vary in length and complexity to convey the written composition meaningfully. Mechanical evaluations in structure are easy to evaluate negatively. Flexibility within the sentence structure itself helps create meaningfulness to the reader. A variety of structured forms is essential to good written communication.

SPELLING – LEXICAL WORDS

The importance of spelling has been a dilemma for teachers when evaluating written composition. It should be noted the spelling is a coordinator of language arts and promotes accurate and effective communication. The message of written communication is primary and spelling is a secondary promoter. Lexical spelling differences caused by phonetic irregularities in English orthography are troublesome in written communication. Dictionary usage needs special attention when spelling accuracy is in question. Accurate spelling, however, promotes good written communication which makes more effective overall communication. Misspelled vocabulary words need special attention through appropriate spelling techniques.

WRITING AS AN ART

Opportunities for the handicapped individual to express ideas that are self-portraitures is a communicative tool of written expression. The revealing of self can take on poetic as well as fictional and nonfictional forms. Special emphasis should be placed on having creative writing edited by the authors themselves. Written structure needs to follow composition styles, accurate syntax, and have good spelling for the sake of the reader. Exceptions should be accepted when it improves the written ideas/messages wished to be conveyed by the writer.

Agencies – Learning Disabilities

Association for Children and Adults with Learning Disabilities
4156 Library Road
Pittsburgh, PA 15234

Council for Learning Disabilities
P.O. Box 40303
Overland Park, KS 66204

National Center for the Learning Disabled
99 Park Avenue, 6th Floor
New York, NY 10016

PHYSICAL DISABILITIES

Definition by P.L. 94-142
    The definition of those individuals receiving federal assistance under the law is:
"Orthopedically Impaired—A severe orthopedic impairment which adversely affects a child's educational performance. The term includes impairments caused by a congenital anomaly (e.g., clubfoot, absence of some limb, etc.), impairments caused by disease (e.g., poliomyelitis, bone tuberculosis, etc.), and impairments from other causes (e.g., cerebral palsy, amputations, and fractures or burns which cause contractures)."

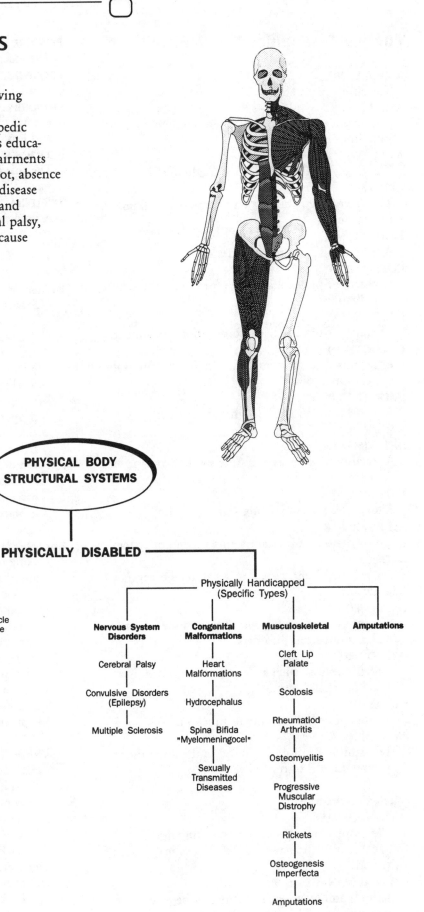

PHYSICAL BODY STRUCTURAL SYSTEMS

PHYSICALLY DISABLED

Incidental Errors
|
none

Functional Errors
- Social Skills
- Learning Skills
- Locomotion
- Fine/Gross Motor
- Posture
- Speech/Language
- Muscle Tone

Physically Handicapped (Specific Types)

Nervous System Disorders

Cerebral Palsy
|
Convulsive Disorders (Epilepsy)
|
Multiple Sclerosis

Congenital Malformations

Heart Malformations
|
Hydrocephalus
|
Spina Bifida "Myelomeningocel"
|
Sexually Transmitted Diseases

Musculoskeletal

Cleft Lip Palate
|
Scolosis
|
Rheumatiod Arthritis
|
Osteomyelitis
|
Progressive Muscular Distrophy
|
Rickets
|
Osteogenesis Imperfecta
|
Amputations

Amputations

Physical Disabilities Terminology

AMBULATORY
The ability to walk.

AMELIA
The absence of a limb(s) through congenital mal-functioning.

AMPUTATION
The removal of parts or the whole limb(s).

ATROPHY
The decreasing in size or wasting away of a limb, organ, etc.

BILATERAL
A term that relates to two sides.

CORRECTIVE THERAPY
A system of physical activities for the rehabilitation of a disability.

DEGENERATIVE
Alteration from better to worse in form or function.

DISLOCATION
Abnormal displacement of a bone in relation to its position in a joint.

EMERGENCY PROTOCOL
A predetermined plan designated for emergency situations.

INFLAMMATION
A reaction of the tissue causing swelling and/or pain.

MONOPLEGIA
A total disability involving a particular limb.

NEUROMOTOR
A disorder of the brain affecting the motor system.

ORDOSIS
The spinal column curves forward in an exaggerated fashion.

ORTHOPEDICS
A branch of medicine concerned with the treatment of musculoskeletal disorders.

ORTHOTICS
Self-help devices, such as braces, to aid the individual in rehabilitation.

PARALYSIS
The loss of or the inability to function.

PARAPLEGIA
The inability of mobility found in the lower limbs or lower section of the body.

PED
Refers to the foot.

PHONOCOMELIA
A developmental abnormality resulting in the attachment of the hand and feet to the main part of the body.

PHYSICAL MANAGEMENT
Methods and techniques specified to be used to lift, carry, handle, and position a physically handicapped person.

POSTURE
The mechanical efficiency of the body parts.

PROSTHESIS
Artificial substitute for any body part.

QUADRIPLEGIA
A total disability of movement affecting both arms and legs of the individual.

SCOLIOSIS
The spinal column curves laterally in an abnormal way.

TRIPLEGIA
A total disability involving three limbs.

Physical Disabilities Checklist

Positioning
- Braces – types
    - short leg
    - long leg
    - long leg with pelvic band
- joints work easily
- workmanship adapted comfortably to individual
- uprights conform to limb
- proper size
- comfortable when in use
- redness of skin goes away 20 minutes after removal
- is limb mobile?
- brace is quiet when in use
- is brace useful?

Prosthetics (artificial substitute for limb)
- using the prosthetics
- use of assistive devices
    - one cane
    - canes
    - crutches
- worn correctly
- accurate in length/size
- does prothesis stay in place?
- is joint bending appropriately?
- is joint quiet when moving?
- is prosthesis in good condition?

Wheelchair
- seat posture for comfort in the chair
    - width
    - depth
    - height/foot rest
    - arm height
    - back height
- mechanical functioning
    - arm panels and locks
    - back (upholstery comfortable with safety belt)
    - seat frame (upholstery comfortable, folds easily)

wheel locks (secure)
large wheels (move securely without wobbling)
casters (swivel easily without excessive play)

Communication Devices
· Typewriter
    electric
    finger cards
    miniature
· Writing aids
    pencil holders
        clay
        Styrofoam
        plastic
    writing frame
    magnetic wrist hold-down
    wrist weights
    head pointer
    forearm splint
· Communication board
    bliss symbols
    English language board
    portable
· Technical aids
    electronic communications system
    computer adapting to strength skills

Functional Involvement

FUNCTIONAL ERRORS

NEUROLOGICAL IMPAIRMENTS

Physical disorders can be traced to functional deficiencies found in the neurological system of the body, namely the brain and spinal cord. When the nervous system is damaged, muscular weakness or paralysis is possible. Special equipment, special procedures, and specific accommodations are necessary and influence the special education accommodation required under P. L. 94-142. Because brain damage may vary, the functioning disorder will become a highly individual problem and needs to be treated with an individual plan involving all areas that are involved.

The diagrams below may indicate possible variables affected. Depending on the location and the amount of damage to the brain and nervous system, any or all of the following disorders may occur.

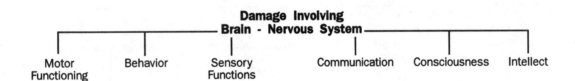

**Damage Involving
Brain - Nervous System**

Motor Functioning   Behavior   Sensory Functions   Communication   Consciousness   Intellect

CEREBRAL PALSY

Etiology	Definition	Classification

Prenatal
  measles-(first three months)
  maternal infection
  RH factor
  heredity
  malnutrition
  drug usage
 	
Perinatal
  lack of oxygen
  breech delivery
  prolonged delivery
 	
Postnatal
  toxic conditions
  infections
  accidents
  tumors
	Cerebral Palsy is created by injury to the brain in motor control areas, usually originating in childhood characterized by paralysis, weakness, and incoordination.	Spasticity-
		increase of muscle tension resulting in continuous increase of resistance to stretching, and jerky, often uncertain movement.
		
		Athetosis-
		continuous involuntary writhing motion.
		 -impaired motor control of hands
		 -impaired speech/swallowing
		
		Ataxia, Rigidity, Tremor-
		lack of motor coordination. Similar to types of seizures.

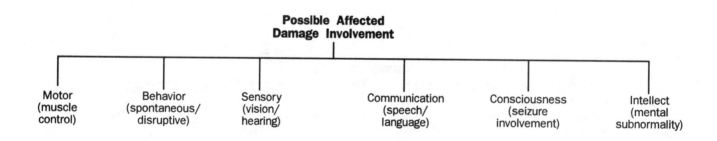

Possible Affected Damage Involvement

Motor (muscle control)

Behavior (spontaneous/ disruptive)

Sensory (vision/ hearing)

Communication (speech/ language)

Consciousness (seizure involvement)

Intellect (mental subnormality)

Surgery	Therapy	Education	Vocational

G O A L S

CONVULSIVE DISORDERS (Epilepsy)

Etiology	Definition	Classification

Head Injury
  motorcycles, car, etc.
 	
Fevers
  meningitis, encephalitis, etc.
 	
Nutrition
 	
Toxic substances
  household chemicals
  (insecticides, fungicides, etc.)
 	
Birth trauma
 	
Prenatal condition
  where mother had injury, illness,
  infections
	An abnormal electrical discharge in the brain where the victim experiences spontaneous and recurring seizures. Twenty types have exhibited themselves differently.	Absence (petit mal)-
		  loss of consciousness, staring,
		  eye-blinking
		Lasts seconds, can have 50 to 100 a day.
		
		Tonic-Clonic (grand mal)-
		  affects whole body which becomes
		  rigid and falls, generalized jerking,
		  frothing at mouth, goes into
		  sleep/coma
		Lasts 3 to 5 minutes.
		
		Complex Partial (psychomotor)-
		  purposeless/stereotypical activity,
		  glassy stare, figits aimlessly, appears
		  intoxicated, garbled language.
		Lasts 2 to 3 minutes.

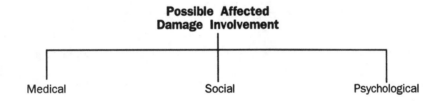

Possible Affected Damage Involvement

Medical   Social   Psychological

Anticonvulsants	Physical Aid During Siezure	Psychological (assurance)	Good Social & Inter-personal Relationship

G O A L S

MULTIPLE SCLEROSIS

Etiology	Definition	Classification
-Unknown Theories -a slow acting virus staying in the body staying in the body for years before illness appears. -defense system attacks its own tissue. -defense system becomes confused when attacking a virus and attacks virus AND body.	The neurons of the central nervous system are insulated with myelin (a fatty substance) which allows the messages to flow freely in the brain. In M.S. the myelin breaks down and forms a scar tissue which blocks or interrupts the flow of the messages to the brain.	Motor movements involving: - eye - paralysis of body parts - hand shaking - bowel/bladder control - slurred speach - gait (staggering/dragging feet) - numbness - loss of coordination

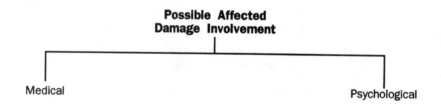

Possible Affected
Damage Involvement

Medical   Psychological

Drug Treatment		Self Help Devices	Diet		Psychological adjustment to motor (paralysis/coordination)
Corti-costeroids	Muscle Relaxant		Liquid	Roughage	

GOALS

70

FUNCTIONAL ERRORS

CONGENITAL MALFORMATIONS

According to the National Center for Clinical Infant Programs, one to two percent of all infants are born with some disabling condition. A genetic defect caused by the chromosomes contributed by the father and/or mother may cause a malformation at conception. During fetal development viruses, bacteria, chemical substances (the list is extensive), may impair the fetus in such a way that certain anomalies occur. Damage of the chromosomes of the parents'—teratogens—may impede normal development. This damage may be caused by those similar conditions that form fetus malformations.

The National Center for Clinical Infant Programming states that 100,000 to 150,000 infants per year may be born with a mental retardation condition. Additional birth malformations causing physical disabilities or specific health problems include cleft lip/palate, congenital heart disorders, cystic fibrosis, muscular dystrophy, and neural tube defects (spina bifida and anencephaly). Fetal Alcohol Syndrome (FAS) is the most frequent cause of teratogenic damage today.

Substance abuse is a rising major cause of congenital malfunctions affecting the fetus. Smoking, alcohol, and other drug usage by mothers during pregnancy have greatly increased the possibility of disabling conditions by the age of five. According to information printed by the National Center for Clinical Infant programs, 11 to 12 per cent of children will qualify for services under P. L. 94-142 and P. L. 91-313.

Alcohol intake during pregnancy may affect the fetus in damaging ways. When a pregnant woman drinks an alcoholic beverage, the concentration of alcohol in the baby's blood stream is that of the mother. The liver of the baby, however, is unable to process the alcohol at the same rate as that of the mother. High concentrations of alcohol stay in the fetus longer, often up to 24 hours. Two major degrees of damage may occur—Fetal Alcohol Syndrome (FAS), and Alcohol-Related Birth Defects (ARBD). FAS and ARBD are one hundred per cent preventable.

Stages of the fetus development during the pregnancy period are affected in different ways. Physical defects are more common during the early stages, while neurological and growth deficiencies are more likely as pregnancy continues. First trimester tissue growth is affected, particularly in the brain. Brain deficiencies include a reduction in size as well as neuron rearrangement. Low birth rate is the result. Second trimester miscarriage is the major risk. The third trimester fetus undergoes rapid and substantial growth. The brain and nervous system are at the greatest risk.

DEFECTS ATTRIBUTED TO F.A.S. AND A.R.B.D.

Physical Body
    Low birth weight
    Physical growth impaired in adulthood
Head
    small head size
    facial disfiguration
Central Nervous System
    mental retardation
    hyperactive (ADHA)
    developmental delays
    learning disabilities
Organs/Body Parts
    muscle
    bone/joint
    heart
    kidney

Prescription and non-prescription drugs taken by the pregnant mother may cause birth defects. Any drug that has an effect on an adult may affect a pregnant woman's fetus because the drug crosses to the fetus through the placenta.

Prescription Drug Intake

Drug	Possible Defects
Tranquilizers (Valium, Librium, etc.)	-cleft palate, heart, nervous system
Skin tissue treatment (Accutane, Teglson)	-birth defects
Aspirin	-perinatal—excessive bleeding

Non-Prescription Drugs

Drug	Defects
Cocaine/crack	-Prenatal—stroke, kidney, limbs, digestive system, nervous system, heart, lungs
	-First year of life—immune system, muscle development, mutations (finger/limb)
	-School years—memory, attention, perception, hyperactive, organizing information

Effects of smoking during pregnancy can have adverse effects on the fetus. During smoking, nicotine, a toxic substance found in cigarettes, crosses the placenta and affects the fetus by constricting placental blood vessels which reduces the supply of oxygen. The inhaling of carbon monoxide while smoking reduces the oxygen carried by the blood. The result is a reduction in healthy development and growth.

The following physical deficiencies may result:
1. Pregnant smoking women have on the average babies seven ounces lighter than non-smoking pregnant women.

2. Smokers have a higher risk of developing bleeding problems because of early separation of placenta, hence a higher rate of miscarriage.
3. Physical and mental growth of children up to seven years of age is impaired.

CONGENITAL EXTREMITIES OF THE BODY

Etiology	Definition	Classification
Genetic Temporary halt in development during first trimester Position of unborn baby in the uterus	A manifested defect caused by the failure of a limb to develop properly, which may take on the absence or malformation of a particular limb(s).	Webbing- in foot or hand-ranging from an extra finger or toe to excess skin/tissue between fingers or toes. Clubfoot- one or both feet are turned at a wrong angle at the ankle. Dislocation of Hip- a malformed socket or head of the thigh or shoulder bone so they fail to join properly. Arthogryposis- joints of a limb are fixed rigid at birth. Amputations- failure of a limb to develop during pregnancy.

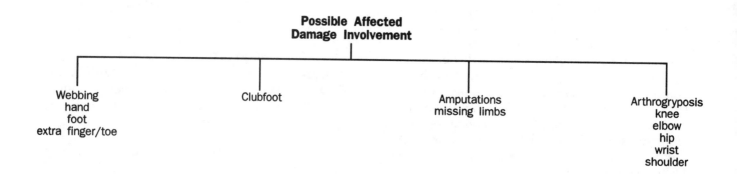

Possible Affected Damage Involvement

Webbing
hand
foot
extra finger/toe

Clubfoot

Amputations
missing limbs

Arthrogryposis
knee
elbow
hip
wrist
shoulder

Prosthesis	Mechanical Problems	Adjustment Problems	Motor Use

G O A L S

CONGENITAL HEART DEFECTS		
Etiology	**Definition**	**Classification**
Unknown causes Heredity Rubella during first trimester	A disorder causing the heart to grow abnormally, originating during the first trimester when the heart is being formed. -Blockage of blood passage from heart to lungs (prenatal) -"hole in the heart" between two upper or lower chambers -aorta may be pinched affecting blood flow -defective valves.	-bluish coloring of the skin -weight loss/improper gains -tiredness, weakness, breathlesness

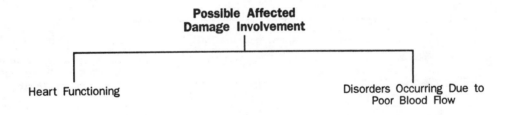

**Possible Affected
Damage Involvement**

Heart Functioning

Disorders Occurring Due to
Poor Blood Flow

Regulation of Physical Activity	Drugs/Mechanical Aids	Emotional Impact on Child/Family
GOALS		

HYDROCEPHALUS		
Etiology	**Definition**	**Classification**
-genetic origin -varies in different geographical areas and seasons -rarely found among Blacks and Chinese -common in Western Europe -inflammation blocking a ventricle caused by bleeding at birth -fetal hemorrhage at birth	An excess of clear, water-like cerebrospinal fluid which circulates through and around the brain. The fluid contains sodium, potassium, calcium, proteins, and other chemicals	Obstructive Hydrocephalus-obstruction that occurs in any of the 4 ventricle passages in the brain from which the cerebrospinal fluid flows into the bloodstream. Fluid pressure builds up against the brain and against the bones of the skull. Arnold-Chiari Malformations-lower part of the brain is deformed causing blockage in the 4th ventricle. Disability is also represented when spina bifida occurs.

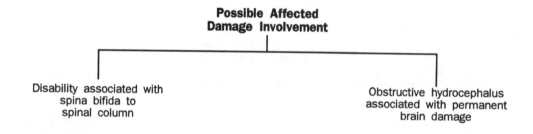

Possible Affected Damage Involvement

Disability associated with spina bifida to spinal column

Obstructive hydrocephalus associated with permanent brain damage

Surgery -corrective (clearing obstruction) -artificial shunt	Mental Subnormality	Physical Development

G O A L S

SPINA BIFIDA		
Etiology	**Definition**	**Classification**
-unknown -occurs during first month of pregnancy	A defect in the spinal column resulting from failure of the spine to close. Spina Bifida Occulta- an opening to one or more vertebrae of the spinal column- no damage to spinal cord. Spina Bifida Manifesta- 1. Meningocele Protective covering has pushed out through vertebrae opining in a sac. Spinal cord not damaged. 2. Myelomeningocele Spinal cord protrudes through the back, forming a sac or exposed tissue/nerves.	-muscle weakness -muscle paralysis -loss of bladder control -loss of feeling below cleft area -depending on degree of mobility emotional/social difficulties

Possible Affected Damage Involvement

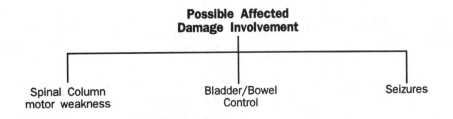

| Spinal Column motor weakness | Bladder/Bowel Control | Seizures |

Series of Operations	Bowel/Bladder Management	Medications	Physical Therapy	Ambulatory Adaptations
GOALS				

SEXUALLY TRANSMITTED DISEASES (STD)

DEFINITION
STDs are organisms (bacteria, fungi, protozoa, and viruses) that are transmitted by close intimate or sexual contact: intercourse. There are twenty identifiable types of STD.

STD (according to prevalency in general population)	Damage Involvement to Individual	Damage Involvement to Fetus	Medical Cures
Gonorrhea	M penis-mucous discharge, blood/pus in feces, infection in rectum, sterility F vagina-mucous discharge, blood/pus in feces, infection in rectum, sterility	Eye disorders	Antibiotics
Syphillis	M/F-Nervous system Heart disease Insanity Brain Damage	Still born Severe illness	Antibiotics
Genital Herpes	Virus related to immune system. F-cancer of the cervix M-sores/blisters on penis/rectum	Still born Severe brain damage	None
Chlamydia trachomatis	Sterility F-pelvic inflammation M-burning/itching while urinating	Premature/Still-born Pneumonia Eye infections	Antibiotics (not Penicillin)
Hepatitis B	M/F-Severe illness Liver damage Death	Premature births/ Spontaneous abortion Born with Type B	No cure

Sexually Transmitted Diseases (STD)
Fetal Damage Incurred

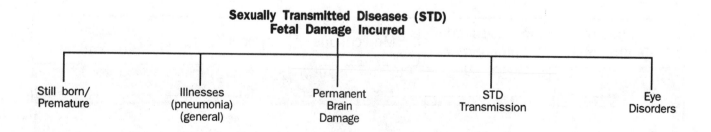

| Still born/ Premature | Illnesses (pneumonia) (general) | Permanent Brain Damage | STD Transmission | Eye Disorders |

FUNCTIONAL ERRORS
MUSCULOSKELETAL DISORDERS

The physical disability relating to the structural inability of the individual to maintain a straight and normal condition is called a musculoskeletal problem. This involves the motor system as well as the skeleton itself. Defects or disease of the muscles and the bones can be considered a qualifying disability under P. L. 94-142, even though the mental and academic abilities of these individuals may not be affected.

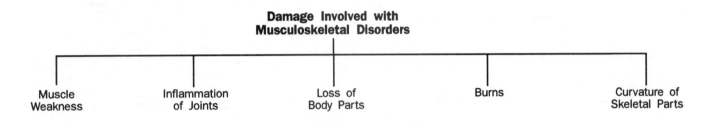

Damage Involved with Musculoskeletal Disorders

| Muscle Weakness | Inflammation of Joints | Loss of Body Parts | Burns | Curvature of Skeletal Parts |

AMPUTATIONS		
Etiology	**Definition**	**Classification**

Accident trauma-
 	
Surgical amputations
	Amputation refers to the absence at birth, or the removal at a later time, of limb(s) or parts thereof.	Traumatic amputation-
		  loss of a limb or body part through an accident.
		
		Surgical amputation-
		  -advanced diabetes
		  -circulatory problems
		  -bone cancers
		
		Congenital-
		  a condition requiring attention at birth because of malformation.

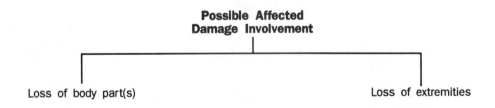

Possible Affected Damage Involvement

| Loss of body part(s) | Loss of extremities |

Prosthesis	Physical Therapy	Emotional Counseling

G O A L S

ARTHRITIS		
Etiology	**Definition**	**Classification**
-unknown -theory: a virus or organism which, when triggered, causes inflammation within the joint structure of the body. (Virus is dormant for a given period.) -tendency that more than one family member may become affected.	Arthritis (inflamation of a joint) is a common term that covers different conditions which cause aching and pain in joints and connective tissues in the musculoskeletal systems. Rheumatism (a part of the disease disorder of arthritis) is a general word used for unexplained aches in muscles.	Juvenile rheumatiod arthritis- a group of diseases causing growth disturbances and resulting in high fever and skin rash. It may cause malformations of body tissue and organs. Crippling is a major problem. Ankylosing spondylitis (rheumatoid spondylitis Marie Strumpell disease)- found in late adolescence among males. It involves back pain, stiffness, loss of spinal mobility due to inflammation of spinal joints.

Possible Affected Damage Involvement

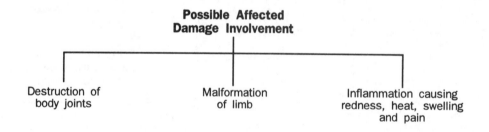

| Destruction of body joints | Malformation of limb | Inflammation causing redness, heat, swelling and pain |

Diet (loss of appetite)	Physical Therapy (exercise & physical aids)	Specialists to assist with emotional/ vocational problems	Medication Program (surgery, medical)	Medication (drugs)

G O A L S

CLEFT LIP/PALATE DISORDER

Etiology	Definition	Classification
-Prenatal condition -Drugs -Disease -Malnutrition -Heredity -Adverse environmental change	Cleft lip is the failure of the two sides of the upper lip to grow together properly before birth. Cleft palate is a split or opening in the roof of the mouth.	Cleft Lip -lower part of the upper lip may be cleft -gap between upper lip and nostril through the upper jaw into the palate. -may appear slightly left/right of face center. Cleft Palate -soft palate (used for swallowing/ speaking) may be clefted. In this case, the back of the mouth is affected. -uvula (the small projection of tissue that hangs from the back of the mouth) is affected. -clefts may extend from soft palate into the hard palate (bony front part of the roof of the mouth). Entire palate from upper jaw to teeth may be affected.

Possible Affected
Damage Involvement

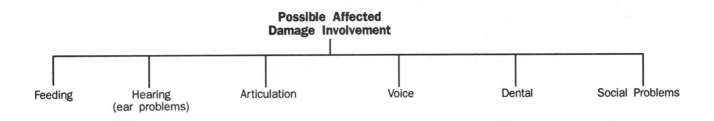

| Feeding | Hearing (ear problems) | Articulation | Voice | Dental | Social Problems |

Adapted feeding techniques	Speech correction	Psychological assistance	Hearing/ear disabilities	Surgery (prosthesis)

G O A L S

OSTEOGENESIS IMPERFECTA

Etiology	Definition	Classification
Inherited disorder apparent at birth through the first few years of life	Osteogenesis imperfecta is a disorder of connective tissue that results primarily in fragile bones that break easily, often called "brittle bones".	Osteogenesis imperfecta tarda- the child appears normal at birth but develops recurring fractures (of limbs) after the first year of life. Congenital osteogenesis impertura tarda- the fractures are present at birth and usually fatal.

Possible Affected Damage Involvement

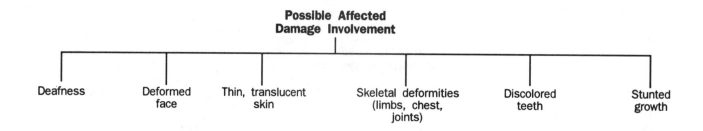

| Deafness | Deformed face | Thin, translucent skin | Skeletal deformities (limbs, chest, joints) | Discolored teeth | Stunted growth |

Wheel Chair	Surgery	Braces

G O A L S

OSTEOMYELITIS		
Etiology	**Definition**	**Classification**
The bacterium (staphylococcus aureus) causes an infection in the bone. Bacteria are carried from an infected site (boil or sore on the surface of the skin) to arm, leg or pelvic bones, or from trauma that results in a wound, fracture or other injury.	Osteomyelitis is an infection of the bone resulting from the growth of germs within the long bone of children.	Osteomyelitis is accompanied by localized pain, tenderness, heat, swelling and restricted movement. Fever or fatigue may accompany these symptoms. Osteomyelitis may then be classified as either chronic or acute, depending on the severity of the infection.

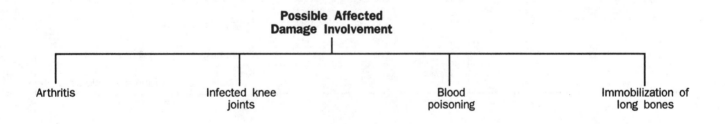

Possible Affected Damage Involvement

Arthritis   Infected knee joints   Blood poisoning   Immobilization of long bones

Medical treatment with antibiotics	Surgery to drain pus from infected bone area	Immobilization
G O A L S		

MUSCULAR DYSTROPHY/ATROPHY

Etiology	Definition	Classification
Inherited disease	**MUSCULAR DYSTROPHY** A heredity disease characterized by progressive weakness caused by a degeneration (breakdown) of muscle cells and their replacement by fat or fibrous tissue. **MUSCULAR ATROPHY** A hereditary disease characterized by progressive weakness caused by neurological damage that causes muscles to become weak.	Duchenne (pseudohypertrophic): -enlargement of some muscle groups (calf muscles). -inherited sex link to male babies. -three to five years (abnormal gait-tendency to fall). -very progressive to wheelchair then death Landouzy Dejernine infection (faciocapulohumeral): -onset in adolescence. -affects muscles of face. -affects shoulder girdles. -unusual smile. -cannot whistle. -closes eyes tightly. -difficulty in raising arms. -usually mild to moderate (seldom dies)

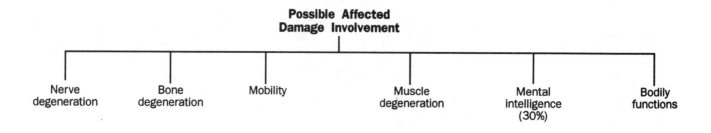

Possible Affected Damage Involvement

Nerve degeneration | Bone degeneration | Mobility | Muscle degeneration | Mental intelligence (30%) | Bodily functions

Physical surgery (wheelchair)	Physiotherapy	Occupational Therapy	Educational Counseling	Diet

GOALS

RICKETS		
Etiology	**Definition**	**Classification**
Vitamin D deficiency	Rickets is caused by a deficiency resulting in a failure of normal calcification	A disease which appears in breast-fed infants who do not receive a vitamin D supplement, or in poor and over-populated areas. It results in bone malformations.

**Possible Affected
Damage Involvement**

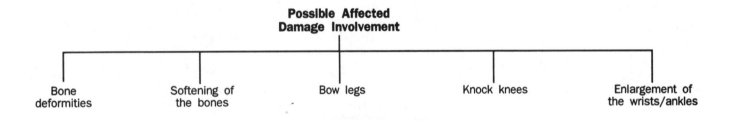

| Bone deformities | Softening of the bones | Bow legs | Knock knees | Enlargement of the wrists/ankles |

Vitamin D / Calcium Supplements

GOAL

SCOLIOSIS		
Etiology	**Definition**	**Classification**
In the majority of cases the cause is unknown. In other cases the cause is congenital or poor posture.	Scoliosis is an abnormal; curvature of the spine which may progress to deformity of the vertebral parts of the spine.	Idiopathic/Infantile- affects infants between birth and 3 years of age, affecting spinal curvature. Juvenile- onset at ages 4 through 10, affecting the curvature. Adolescent- onset 10 and over affecting skeletal maturity. Scoliosis/Myelomeningocele (spina bifida)- scoliosis is an accompanying condition that may result from the deformity spinal myelomeningocele.

**Possible Affected
Damage Involvement**

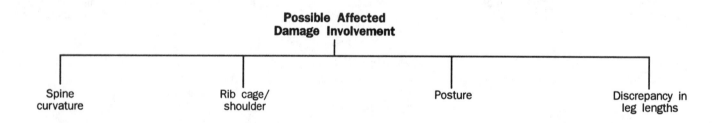

Spine curvature   Rib cage/ shoulder   Posture   Discrepancy in leg lengths

Exercise	Corrective surgery	Brace

G O A L S

SPECIALIZED HEALTH IMPAIRMENT PROBLEMS

These are two major categories listed for services with those having health problems that require special services in the educational program. Health impairments are those problems that ar associated with the category of physical disabilities. "Specialized Health Care Needs" is a new category adopted by the Council for Exceptional Children as needing special educational adaptation to the typical school day.

Technology has provided children with specialized life and/or health support so that education in the school site is now possible and appropriate. Specialized individual education programs are being planned and augmented to meet the medical and academic needs of these students. Although school equipment and/or curriculum may need to be changed or altered, academic pursuits are available and should be considered necessary and right even though this is introduced for the first time.

"Specialized Health Care Needs" category requires specialized technological health procedures for life support and/or health support during the school day. These students may or may not require special education. There is a similarity between these individuals and those having physical and health impairments; however, these children are considered medically fragile and technologically dependent. They require intensive and long term care.

Those students who benefit from this program have special medical needs which affect their learning potential. Some of the conditions included for service by the schools are ventilator dependence, tracheotomy dependence, oxygen dependence, nutritional supplement dependence, congestive heart problems, need for high-technology care, monitoring and/or kidney dialysis. Fatigue, limited vitality, short attention span, and limited mobility may affect these students so that educational adjustment is needed.

Although environmental changes are imperative, intellectual changes are seldom required, and these individuals should not be allowed to be placed where instructional programming is below the grade level for their mental ability.

SPECIAL HEALTH IMPAIRMENTS

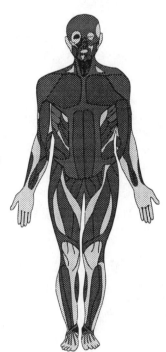

Special Health Impairments refers to health problems that dictate the need for special medical or educational services. Any chronic or acute health problem that limits strength, vitality, or alertness which adversely affects the educational programming is included in this category. Health conditions involved include the body organs, metabolic problems, circulatory problems, and other miscellaneous type disorders.

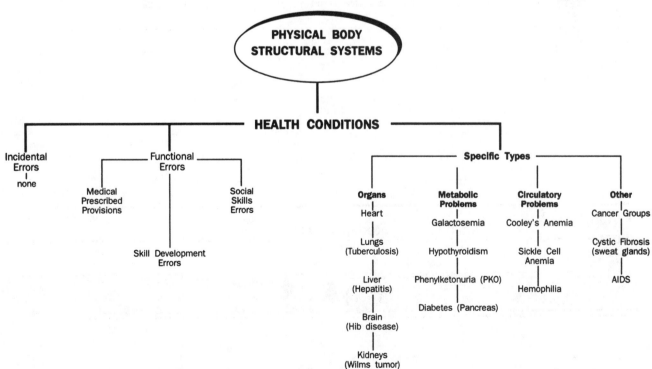

PHYSICAL BODY STRUCTURAL SYSTEMS

HEALTH CONDITIONS

Incidental Errors
- none

Functional Errors
- Medical Prescribed Provisions
- Skill Development Errors
- Social Skills Errors

Specific Types

Organs
- Heart
- Lungs (Tuberculosis)
- Liver (Hepatitis)
- Brain (Hib disease)
- Kidneys (Wilms tumor)

Metabolic Problems
- Galactosemia
- Hypothyroidism
- Phenylketonuria (PKO)
- Diabetes (Pancreas)

Circulatory Problems
- Cooley's Anemia
- Sickle Cell Anemia
- Hemophilia

Other
- Cancer Groups
- Cystic Fibrosis (sweat glands)
- AIDS

Incidental Involvement
FUNCTIONAL ERRORS

HEART (Rheumatic Heart Disease)		
Etiology	**Definition**	**Classification**
-inflammation caused by streptococcal infection; often called rheumatic fever	Rheumatic heart disease results when a valve has formed scar tissue that blocks the normal flow of blood through the heart.	Rheumatic heart disease is the product of an inflammation of iether or both valves on the left side of the heart. As the inflammation subsides, the valve heals by forming scar tissue that prevents the valve from opening and closing properly. The normal flow of the heart is disrupted

Possible Affected
Damage Involvement

Arthritis of joints   Quality of life   Permanent heart damage

Prophylaxis (reocurrences possible)	Antibiotic Therapy	Reduced active lifestyle	Surgery	Counselling
GOALS				

LUNGS (Asthma)		
Etiology	**Definition**	**Classification**
Asthma is a response to: -an allergic reaction to the environment -an emotional response in itself -a family pattern	Asthma is characterized by wheezing and coughing due to a spasmodic contraction in the bronchi.	Caused by three changes in the lungs: -Bronchoconstriction muscles wrapped around the bronchial tubes tighten -Edema the lining of the bronchial tubes swells -Extra mucus is made in the bronchial tubes reducing the size of the airways and the amount of air that can move in and out of the bronchial tubes.

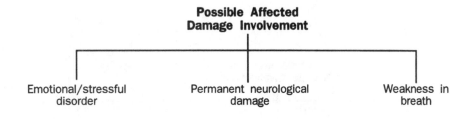

Possible Affected Damage Involvement

Emotional/stressful disorder   Permanent neurological damage   Weakness in breath

Learn control of attacks	Drugs control	Regulation of physical activity	Counselling of fear while in the attack
G O A L S			

LIVER (Reye's Syndrome)

Etiology	Definition	Classification

A two-stage disease:
 	
Stage One-
Associated with previous viral infection (flu, chickenpox, colds)
 	
Stage Two-
infracranial pressure to the brain-hypoglycemia, fatty infiltration of the liver, encephalopathy
 	
Association with use of aspirin while treating viral infections.
	Reye's syndrome is a child's disease affecting all organs of the body, but its main targets are the liver and the brain. It causes increasing pressure within the brain, massive accumulations of fat in the liver and in other body organs.	Reye's syndrome has common symptoms with many diseases.
		
		Stage One:
		-persistent vomiting
		-brain dysfunction
		  lifelessness
		  loss of energy
		  drowsiness
		
		Stage Two:
		-personality changes
		  irritability
		  aggressive
		-disorientation
		  confusion
		  irrational behavior
		-delirium, convulsions

Possible Affected Damage Involvement

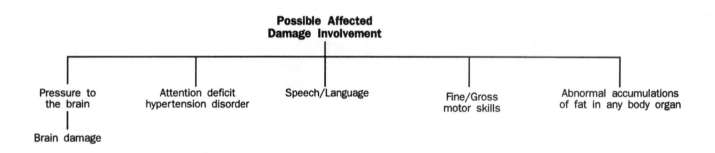

| Pressure to the brain | Attention deficit hypertension disorder | Speech/Language | Fine/Gross motor skills | Abnormal accumulations of fat in any body organ |

Brain damage

Brain therapy	Psychological consultation	Neuropsychological consultation	Liver function tests are essential

GOALS

KIDNEYS		
Etiology	**Definition**	**Classification**
-abnormal rudimentary tissue in and around the kidney.	Kidney neoplasm is a kidney tumor which may affect the function of the organ and must be treated by surgery, hemotherapy, and radiotherapy.	Kidney neoplasms- nephroblastoma (Wilm's tumor)- a growth which becomes apparent as a lump in the abdominal area, which can spread to nearby tissues and also into the bloodstream to other area organs.

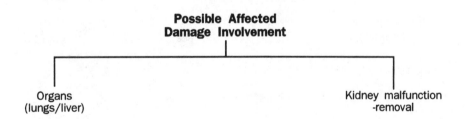

Possible Affected Damage Involvement

Organs (lungs/liver)

Kidney malfunction -removal

Transplant	Immunosuppressive medications	Dialysis
G O A L S		

Functional Involvement
FUNCTIONAL ERRORS

METABOLIC PROBLEMS

GALACTOSEMIA		
Etiology	**Definition**	**Classification**
-a genetic disorder caused by the combination of defective recessive genes affecting the metabolic system	The body's failure to break down a special sugar in milk called galactose.	A genetic metabolic disorder that creats an enzyme deficiency affecting the body's ability to metabolize galactose. Symptoms include convulsions, jaundice, and feeding difficulties

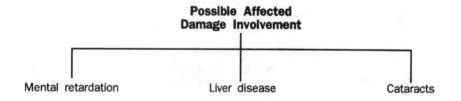

Possible Affected
Damage Involvement

Mental retardation   Liver disease   Cataracts

Treatment-Exclusion of milk from diet	Avert mental retardation or treat mentally retarded disorders
G O A L S	

HYPOTHYROIDISM		
Etiology	**Definition**	**Classification**
-inherited deficiency causing improper thyroid hormone production	Hypothyroidism occurs when an infant is born with lack of a thyroid gland or with an underactive thyroid gland.	A congenital problem that produces various types of disorders affecting intellectual and normal body functioning if not detected within the first 24 hours after birth. Symptoms include sluggishness, constipation, and poor growth.

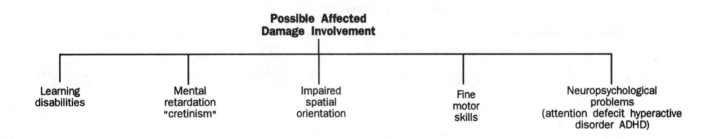

Possible Affected Damage Involvement

Learning disabilities

Mental retardation "cretinism"

Impaired spatial orientation

Fine motor skills

Neuropsychological problems (attention defecit hyperactive disorder ADHD)

Clinical diagnosis with testing on first day of life	Control intake of thyroid for normal body need

G O A L S

PHENYLKETONURIA (PKU)

Etiology	Definition	Classification
A genetic disorder caused by a combination of defective recessive genes affecting the metabolic system.	Phenylketonuria is a functional disorder ocurring when an individual is unable to metabolize amino acid - phenylanaline to tyrosine.	PKU affects the normal growth and development of the newborn infant, thus requiring artificial control of metabolizing the amino acids. Failure to control leads to external brain and neurological types of disorders.

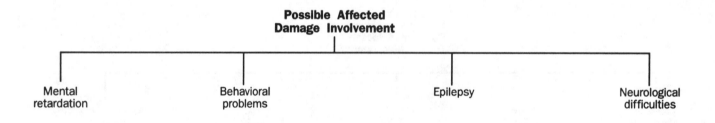

Possible Affected Damage Involvement

Mental retardation   Behavioral problems   Epilepsy   Neurological difficulties

Diet	Clinical diagnosis with testing for disfunction at birth	Urea cycle metabolism testing	Genetic testing	Neurological types of disorders

G O A L S

PANCREAS (Diabetes)		
Etiology	**Definition**	**Classification**
-tendency is present at birth -viruses participate in malfunction (not contagious) -excessive fat intake causing obesity -autoimmunity (process where body attacks its own cells)	Diabetes is a disease in which the body does not produce or properly use insulin, a hormone that is needed to convert sugar, starches, and other foods into the energy needed for daily life.	-Type 1 Diabetes (insulin dependent) The pancreas stops making the hormone insulin or makes only an inadequate amount for body use. Insulin must be artificially inserted into the body, preferrably the bloodstream. -Secondary Diabetes Damage to the pancreas from chemicals, certain medicines, or diseases of the pancreas.

**Possible Affected
Damage Involvement**

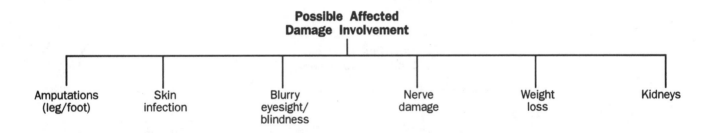

| Amputations (leg/foot) | Skin infection | Blurry eyesight/ blindness | Nerve damage | Weight loss | Kidneys |

Insulin intake (pills - shots)	Blood pressure control	Special care of body parts (feet, skin, teeth)	Reduce stress	Exercise	No salt intake
G O A L S					

Functional Involvement
FUNCTIONAL ERRORS

CIRCULATORY PROBLEMS

THALASSEMIA (Cooley's Anemia)		
Etiology	**Definition**	**Classification**
-genetic disorder with both parents carrying the trait	In thalassemia, the red blood cells are pale because they contain less red coloring material (hemoglobin) than normal. Paleness, weakness, irritability, and failure to thrive are included as the earliest warning signs.	Hemoglobin is a protein pigment of the red blood cells that carries oxygen to the tissues. Hemoglobin is made up of 4 globin chains. The defect occurs with a decrease or absence of the synthesis of one or more of the globin chains.

**Possible Affected
Damage Involvement**

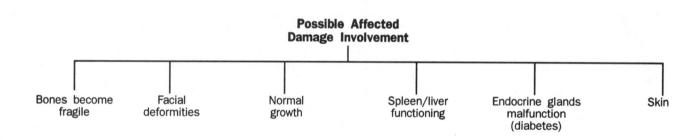

| Bones become fragile | Facial deformities | Normal growth | Spleen/liver functioning | Endocrine glands malfunction (diabetes) | Skin |

Medical emphasis (transfusions)	Bone marrow transplants	Genetic counselling

G O A L S

94

SICKLE CELL ANEMIA

Etiology	Definition	Classification
-a sickle cell gene is inherited from one parent, and a normal gene from the other	Sickle cell anemia is a blood disease where the round blood cells take the shape of a sickle or crescent moon. Almost all of the hemoglobin in the blood is Hbs with no normal adult hemoglobin produced.	Oxygen fails to get throught the small blood vessels because of the abnormal shape of the blood cells, thus causing malfunction of affected areas. Victims get pale, tired, and short of breath. They have bouts of pain in their arms, legs, back and abdomen. Eyes turn yellowish, joints swell up, physical exercise is slowed and the victim has a low resistance to infection.

Possible Affected
Damage Involvement

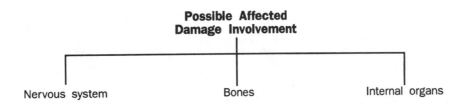

Nervous system   Bones   Internal organs

Control of pain	Medical provisions (penicillin, "low salt", bone marrow transplant)	Increase fetal hemoglobin

G O A L S

HEMOPHILIA		
Etiology	**Definition**	**Classification**
-sex linked disorder transmitted through a recessive gene carried by the mother to male offspring (recently some females have been identified as having the problem when the mother is a carrier and the father has hemophilia).	Hemophilia encompasses at least eight different bleeding disorders that are caused by the lack of any one of ten different blood clotting factors.	The three major severities involved in the problem are: -prolonged bleeding occurs with surgery, tooth extraction, and major injury -bleeding occurs in joints or muscles following minor trauma (sprain, bump) -bleeding may occur in muscles, joints and body organs with no apparent cause or injury.

Possible Affected Damage Involvement

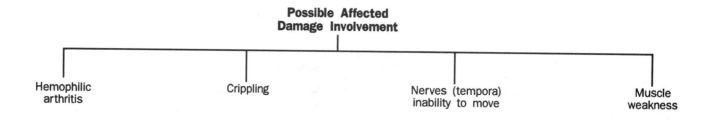

| Hemophilic arthritis | Crippling | Nerves (tempora) inability to move | Muscle weakness |

Intravenous infusion	Avoid trauma	No aspirin	Educational adjustments

G O A L S

AIDS		
Etiology	**Definition**	**Classification**

-virus transmitted by
  -sexual contact
  -intravenous drug abusers
  -transfusions
  -pregnancy
	AIDS is a defect in an individual's natural immunity against disease. A virus attacks the white blood cells that protect the body from infection.	A pregnant woman infected with AIDS can pass the virus to her unborn child because of close contact between the mother's bloodstream and the infant's. The infant becomes extremely ill when born. A child needing a transfusion may contract the virus through the donated blood.

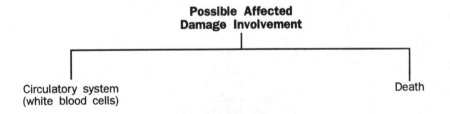

**Possible Affected
Damage Involvement**

Circulatory system
(white blood cells)   Death

Attend school when permitted by professional	Counselling	Medical attention
G O A L S		

MISCELLANEOUS

CANCER		
Etiology	**Definition**	**Classification**
Unknown-particularly in children	Cancer is a GROUP of diseases occurring when a particular cell or group of cells begin to multiply and grow uncontrollably, crowding out the normal cells	see below

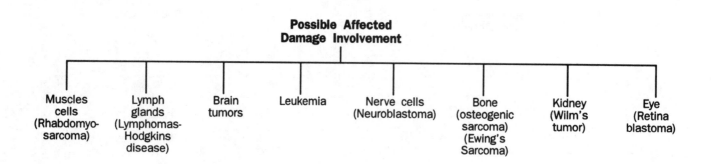

Possible Affected
Damage Involvement

Muscles cells (Rhabdomyosarcoma)   Lymph glands (Lymphomas-Hodgkins disease)   Brain tumors   Leukemia   Nerve cells (Neuroblastoma)   Bone (osteogenic sarcoma) (Ewing's Sarcoma)   Kidney (Wilm's tumor)   Eye (Retina blastoma)

CLASSIFICATION

Leukemia
- originates in the blood and develops in the bone marrow
- certain white blood cells escape normal control remaining young and multiplying rather than going through their aging process
- a leukemic blast (immature stage in cellular development) spills in bone marrow

Lymphomas - Hodgkin's disease
- a circulatory system where vessels carry lymph (a colorless fluid found in many body tissues)
- lymphoid organs including lymph nodes, spleen, thymus, used to produce and store infection fighting cells
- organs including tonsils, stomach, small intestine, skin
- swelling and pain in neck, armpit, or groin

Brain tumors
- occurs from 5-10 years of age to adult
- accompanying headaches, vomiting, lethargy
- diagnosis by brain scan - CAT SCAN

Neuroblastoma
- young nerve cells develop abnormally
- location in the adrenal glands located near the kidneys
- diagnosis by urine
- symptoms include listlessness, diarrhea, pain in abdomen

Wilns tumor
- kidney cancer
- symptoms in swelling or lump in abdomen; fever, pain
- diagnosis by X-ray or CAT SCAN

Retinoblastoma
- rare cancer of the eye
- found by ophthalmoscope examination

Rhabdomyosarcoma (rhabdosarcoma)
- soft tissue sarcoma arising from muscle cells
- found in head and neck area, pelvic, extremities
- symptoms include a noticeable lump/swelling
- diagnosis by biopsy

Osteogenic (Ewing's) sarcoma
- Osteogenic is the ends of bones involved in large bones
- symptoms include pain and swelling
- diagnosis by x-ray
- Ewing's affects the bone shaft
- symptoms include fever, chills, weakness

Hospitalization	Surgery	Chemotherapy	Radiation therapy
G O A L S			

CYSTIC FIBROSIS (CF)

Etiology	Definition	Classification
-an unidentified inherited chromosomal problem involving a CF gene coming from each parent. -such circumstances do not assure automatic cystic fibrosis.	CF is a disorder of certain glands of the body; predominantly the sweat and mucous glands, which function abnormally producing salty sweat and overly thick mucous.	Glandular disorder involving: Mucous Glands -blockage of the airways in the lungs with thick mucous leads to coughing spells, wheezing, and difficult breathing. -mucous plugs the tiny ducts of the pancreas causing improper digestive chemical secretion. Sweat Glands -loss of salt causes discomfort such as abdominal pain and exhaustion, but usually no permanent damage since diet is supplemented by salt intake.

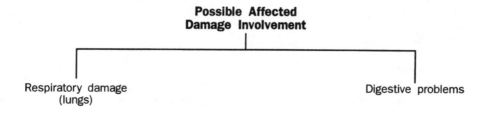

Possible Affected Damage Involvement

Respiratory damage (lungs)

Digestive problems

Chest physical therapy	Diet (enzyme supplement)	Antibiotic therapy

GOALS

MOTOR DEVELOPMENT

Under the law P.L. 94-142 the planning for an individualized educational program includes specialized personnel in physical and motor development of the handicapped individual. The law defines it as:

Physical and motor fitness: fundamental motor skills and patterns; and skills in aquatics, dance, and individual and group games and sports (including intramural and lifetime sports). The term includes special and physical education, educational movement, and motor development.

The performance of motor functions includes the basic motor functions, the ability to perform motor functions, and skill competencies. The individual's designated plan must identify the strengths and weaknesses in motor and physical fitness development and decide on annual goals with short term objectives for implementation in a planned educational setting or environment.

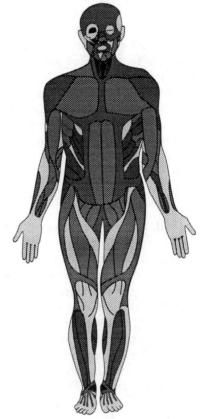

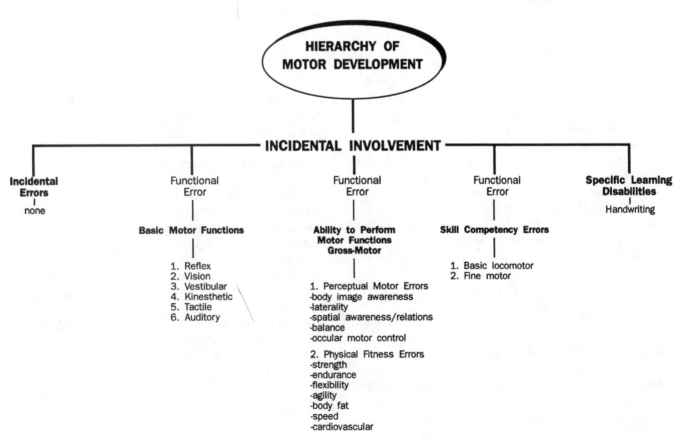

HIERARCHY OF MOTOR DEVELOPMENT

INCIDENTAL INVOLVEMENT

Incidental Errors
| none

Functional Error

Basic Motor Functions
1. Reflex
2. Vision
3. Vestibular
4. Kinesthetic
5. Tactile
6. Auditory

Functional Error

Ability to Perform Motor Functions Gross-Motor

1. Perceptual Motor Errors
-body image awareness
-laterality
-spatial awareness/relations
-balance
-occular motor control

2. Physical Fitness Errors
-strength
-endurance
-flexibility
-agility
-body fat
-speed
-cardiovascular

Functional Error

Skill Competency Errors
1. Basic locomotor
2. Fine motor

Specific Learning Disabilities
Handwriting

BASIC MOTOR FUNCTIONS

The basic motor functions are dependent on the ability for the sensory receptive system to be intact and operate. These systems take information through their respective senses and send that information to the central nervous system. The basic component is movement. Both controlled and spontaneous movement are involved.

If the movement process is unable to perform its appropriate functioning, the individual may have difficulty in obtaining the necessary information for processing efficiently and effectively.

MOTOR LEARNING VOCABULARY

Motor Skill: Ability to control and direct the voluntary muscle of the body.

Motor Learning: A somewhat permanent change in a motor skill resulting from practice or past experience. Learning of movement-oriented skills.

Perceptual-Motor: Ability to interpret, select, and organize types of sensory information that may be present for the act of performance.

Perceptions: Receiving of input or stimuli into the body by the senses (taste, touch, sight, sound, hearing).

Gross Motor: The acquisition of physical skills and fitness by
output or responsive movements of the large body muscle groups.

Fine Motor: The acquisition of control over body extremities by output or responsive movements of the smaller muscles of the body (eyes and fingers).

Skill: A common motor activity with a general goal.

Auditory Motor: Movement resulting from cues/stimuli dealing with hearing-listening.

Visual Motor: Movement resulting from clues/stimuli dealing with seeing; handwriting, math, and physical education academic areas are influenced.

Psychomotor Learning: A somewhat permanent change in performance of a motor skill.

Motor Control: The internal processes operating under specific performance conditions.

Movement: A change in position of any part of the body.

Motor Pattern: A designated plan of movement used in the performance of a fundamental skill.

Form: A complete pattern of events that completes a motor task.

Performance: An act involving the completion of a motor activity.

Midline Axis: Vertical axis involving the coordination of the two sides of the body.

Developmental Delay: Arrested or retarded states of performance that hinder a particular task from being completed.

Functional Involvement

FUNCTIONAL ERRORS

BASIC MOTOR FUNCTIONS

Perceptual-motor abilities and motor skills are built about the normal development of the basic input systems. These motor skills normally develop through the first five years of life. Sensations arising from the vestibular, visual, kinesthetic, tactile, reflex, and auditory systems must function separately or in combination for successful psycho-motor abilities or motor skills to develop. When these functions fail, development delays are caused. If, by the time the child is 12 years of age, these delays are still present, an adjusted program should be started.

"Developmental disability" is defined in P.L. 95-602, the Rehabilitation, Comprehensive Services, and Developmental Disabilities Amendment of 1978. A chronic disability is likely to continue indefinitely, hence a there is a need for alternate learning patterns or channels. Substantial functional limitations of major life activity include: (1) self-care, (2) receptive and expressive language, (3) learning, (4) mobility, (5) self-direction, (6) capacity for independent living, and (7) economic self-sufficiency. When the person's need reflects a combination or sequence of special, interdisciplinary, or generic care, treatment, or other services, an individual plan and coordination is required by law.

VISION

The sensory processing of environmental information is accomplished by the eyes as they discriminate and identify the objects for use by the individual. The eye is a basic tool for learning and understanding to be accomplished. Refractive and orthoptic vision processes the light rays as they enter the eye. Eye problems, such as near-sighted, far-sighted, and astigmatism result when the rays are not bent properly. Orthoptic vision requires the eye and the muscles to function as a team, otherwise problems in depth perception occur.

Visual perception involves the eye locating an object by reception of light stimuli and formulating an image which crosses the retina. The visual image takes an organizational change and becomes explicit. An exact model, including both depth and surface perception, emerges through visual stimuli.

INTERNEUROSENSORY PROCESSING

Visual/Motor: Ability to fixate on and visually track moving objects; ability to match visual input with appropriate motor responses.

Visual Auditory: Ability to match a sound sensation with a visual image.

Visual/Kinesthetic: The use of motor skills by drawing appropriate visual images.

Visual/Tactile: The ability to visualize an object through touch.

Checklist

· Reversal of letters (b,d; p,q; u,n, etc.) after eight years of age
· Numbers inverted and reversed
· Problems in using right-left orientation
· Trips over or bumps into objects (movement difficulties)
· Poor coordination
· Attention deficit disorder with hyperactivity
· Poor motor skills (handwriting, art work, drawing)
· In testing he/she fails by not writing down answers (oral answer responses correct)
· Appears bright but test poorly
· Concept of time and space is poor

AUDITORY

The sensory process involving the detection and analysis of incoming information patterns of an acoustical nature is called auditory reception. This acoustical process involves the interpretation of the meaning of sound (music-noise) called sound acuity. The interpretation of sound variations in pressure as well as a function in time is auditory discrimination.

The three basic auditory processing parts include the outer, middle, and inner ear. The outer ear localizes sound sources and intensifies certain of these sources. The middle ear acts as a mechanical transformer that increases acoustical efficiency. The inner ear contains the organ of hearing which sends messages to the brain. The inner ear also accelerates and maintains balance as well.

Sound awareness involves the following processes:
· Discrimination as to what is sound versus no sound.
· Localization of a period involving the position of the source and its direction of movement follows.
· Sequential memory of sound patterns are processed according to pitch, rhythm, melody, or speech.
· Acoustical decisions must be made as to the relevancy of the sound selection, sometimes referred to as figure ground discrimination.

INTERNEUROSENSORY PROCESSING

Auditory/visual: Ability to match a sound sensation with a visual image.

Auditory/tactile: Ability to identify through sound sensation objects, shapes, sizes, and forms.

Checklist

· Fails to listen
· Pretends to understand
· Poor receptive vocabulary
· Can't carry out directions
· Can't identify sounds
· Confuses likenesses/differences in sound
· Confuses sounds of letters
· Confuses blends of sounds
· Sequences sounds/syllables in odd manner
· Uses small words incorrectly

KINESTHETIC PROCESSING

Kinesthetic sensory processing in the environment involves purposeful movement of a particular activity in which a relationship occurs. This motor movement varies due to the resistance to movement of the object involved in the action.

The joints, muscles, and tendons throughout the body are involved in limb movement (handwriting included), manipulative tasks, and position of the limbs in space.

Kinesthetic sensory processing mediates elementary locomotor skills as well. These movements bring about change in location such as walking, running, and crawling. The movement process is generally unconscious by nature, implementing the use of both gross and fine motor skills in learning-type situations.

INTERNEUROSENSORY PROCESSING

Kinesthetic/Visual: The use of motor skills by drawing appropriate visual images.

Checklist

· Inability to copy words from chalkboard to paper
· Difficulty in hopping, skipping, hitting a ball
· Difficulty in cutting, pasting, coloring
· Can dictate a story but can't write it
· Can point to spelling but not write it
· Visual tracking difficulty in reading
· Inability to perform a movement on one side of body without unwanted movements on other side
· Uses right hand, right eye, right foot consistently for delegated activities
· Uses inappropriate spacing between words

TACTILE

The tactile sensory receptive processing in the environment involves the ability to perceive dimensions of an object through touch. The tactile system is made up of two subsystems: protective and discriminative. The protective system protects the child from danger. The behavior may result in avoidance or defensiveness by action.

The discriminative subsystem involves the ordering and sorting of sensory stimuli. Functionally, the tactile system aids planned purposeful movement such as handwriting, aids in eye-hand performance activities, and enhances shape and object discrimination. Tactile responses are sensitive to where the body/body parts end and space begins. Such responses can discriminate between the quantity and quality characteristics of a given object when processing information.

INTERNEUROSENSORY PROCESSING

Tactile/Visual: The ability to visualize an object through feeling.
Tactile/Auditory: Ability to identify through sound sensation object's shape, size, and form.

Checklist

· Has trouble sitting in a chair
· Poor handwriting skills
· Has difficulty with likenesses or differences between several objects
· Has difficulty copying from a chalkboard onto paper
· Tends to be distracted in work
· Has difficulty describing the texture of a particular material
· Does not like to be touched
· Tendency to curl fingers and toes when creeping
· Has difficulty calculating size
· Dislikes activities involving touching, such as hugging

REFLEXES

Reflexes are the development of innate responses found functioning at birth. These involuntary movements progressively develop from primitive reflexes to equilibrium and automatic movements. Failure of the reflexes to respond creates developmental delays and causes the individual difficulty with the development of movement and/or motor skills. These difficulties qualify for special assistance under Public Law 99-457.

Primitive reflexes are a series of reflexes that appear and disappear during the first year of life. These 14 reflex movements are responsible for patterns of posture, general movement, the lifting of the head, the ability to balance on all fours, sit, and turn head to outstretched hands. Failure of development of these movements leads to the "clumsy" child category.

Equilibrium movement begins to appear at about nine months. As these 22 reflexes become automatic patterns of movement that influence motor skills usage, the primitive reflexes will disappear. Failure to appear after the first year usually means total nonappearance and causes developmental delays in both sensory and motor skills development. The purpose of equilibrium reflexes include: (1) protection of head and upper body from falling, (2) the maintenance of accurate upright posture, and (3) to control movement necessary for walking, running, jumping, as well as other active movement patterns.

Checklist

PRIMITIVE REFLEXES
· Trouble with sitting up
· Difficulty in maintaining head position
· Trouble with crawling, creeping
· Difficulty in turning the head
· Inability to maintain a sitting posture
· Failure to coordinate head with throwing an object

EQUILIBRIUM REFLEXES
· Poor posture position
· Falls easily, hurting head/arms/neck/shoulders
· Inability to run effectively
· Can't balance on hands/knees
· Has difficulty in touching body parts with the chin
· Has difficulty in maintaining balance with quick change

VESTIBULAR SYSTEM

The vestibular receiving mechanism monitors body movement, detects motions, and regulates the level of awareness in relation to spacing of an object.

Located in the inner ear, the vestibular system sends information concerning movement of the body to the brain (cerebellum/brain stem), to the ocular muscles of the eye, to the stomach, and down the spinal column. It aids reflexes in assisting and maintaining the head in a stable condition. There are two major types of vestibular disorders: Benign Paroxysmal Positional Nystagmus (BPPN) and Perilymph Fistulus (PLFS).

BPPN damage produces distortion in the memory messages sent from the balance organs to the brain. BPPN is caused by head trauma which damages the semicircular canal and associated balance organs of the inner ear. It varies widely in degree but generally worsens in certain positions, especially when the head is positioned back and turned to the affected side. Visual problems include eye muscle fatigue, headaches, focusing, memory and concentration problems, motion sickness, and disorientation in darkness may result. Additional problems include miserable type symptoms such as dizziness, vertigo, nausea, fatigue, and anxiety.

When the tiny membranes that separate the fluid-filled inner ear from the air-filled middle ear break or leak (Perilymph Fistulus), the normal vestibular sensory monitoring is interrupted. Symptoms similar to BPPN occur, such as vertigo, nausea, etc. Hearing loss may result from the fluctuations in hearing and the fullness and pressure in the ears. Diagnosis and surgical repair for this disorder need to be immediate or permanent losses will result.

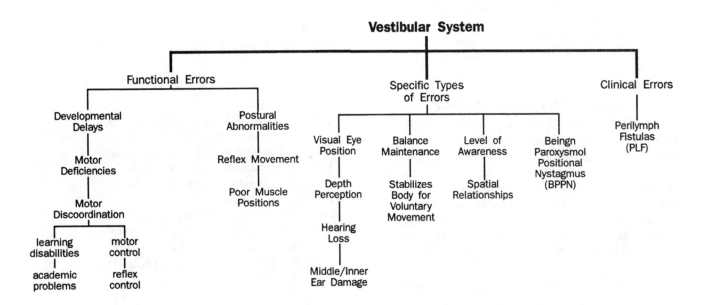

Checklist

· Balance on one foot
· Inability to walk heel to toes
· Inefficient walking, running patterns
· Inability to hop/skip
· Letter spacing when writing
· Inability to reproduce pattern in written form
· Problem in hearing (see auditory Checklist in this section)
· Poor posture (sitting, standing, etc.)
· Poor attention skills
· In constant movement (fidgeting, etc.)

The vestibular system is so involved with all sensory receptive impulses that it is difficult to separate the interrelationships. This whole section is important in understanding how it relates to the development of motor and sensory abilities and the performance of those skills. Little information is available and much research is being done to realize its significance, particularly in deficiencies in academic learning.

Functional Involvement

FUNCTIONAL ERRORS

Performance of Motor Skills

SPLINTER SKILLS

A splinter skill is an expressive motor or a perceptual act that is performed in isolation. It does not generalize to other areas of performance. Splinter skills can possibly be taught if there is damage to a particular sensory input system(s). Generally, remediation takes place through academic learning of a skill rather than a motor skill performance. Balance, laterality, spatial relations, ocular motor control, cross lateral integration and body awareness are included as perceptual motor output acts that may be taught in isolation.

BALANCE – "EQUILIBRIUM"

Balance is the ability to maintain an equilibrium state in a static or dynamic state. It is the zero point for all spatial interpretations and exploration of space. When in a moving position (dynamic), it is the ability to have body control while moving. In the held position (static), it is maintaining equilibrium in a specific position for a given period of time. Balance is the foundation for integrating the two sides of the body and the development of left-right sidedness.

Basic Input Sensory Systems Involvement

VESTIBULAR
VISUAL
REFLEX
KINESTHETIC

Checklist

· Difficulty holding a book
· Difficulty in forming letters in handwriting
· Difficulty in placing blocks one on top of the other
· Difficulty writing on chalkboard
· Difficulty carrying lunch tray to seat
· Seems sloppy
· Falls off seat
· Fails to pay attention in learning setting
· Inability to stand on one foot
· Trips or falls easily

LATERALITY

Laterality is the awareness of the difference between the two sides of the body. Laterality is necessary for the acquisition of balance and equilibrium about the midline of the body which is the vertical axis that involves the coordination of the two body sides. The externalizing of laterality is called directionality.

Directionality is the placing of left and right in space. The control of the eyes directs the development of directionality as well as controls proper spacing.

Basic Input Sensory Systems Involvement

KINESTHETIC
VESTIBULAR (BALANCE)

Checklist

· Proper spacing of letters in handwriting
· Difficulty reading from left to right
· Problem locating a given place in a book
· Inability in pointing to what is right/left of a particular object in a picture
· Avoids use of one side of the body
· Lacks establishment of arm/leg preference
· Walks sideways in one direction better than another
· Uses one extremity more than the other
· Has trouble bouncing/kicking a ball
· Finds it difficult to crawl/creep

SPATIAL RELATIONS – "POSITION IN SPACE"

The spatial system's emphasis is on the body position and its perception of the position of objects in the immediate or distant environment. The child needs to integrate body sensations from his/her environment and make judgements about position, size, and distance of those objects. Awareness of position in space is learned after the child has mastered his/her body in space, attainment of free movement, and the ability to avoid objects.

Basic Input Sensory Systems Involvement

TACTILE
KINESTHETIC
VISUAL
VESTIBULAR

CONCEPT DIFFICULTIES
Direction
· Up–down
· Right–left
· Nearer–further
· Higher–lower

Position
· On–off
· Top–bottom
· In front–behind
· Near–distant

Time
· Now–later
· Before–after
· Morning–afternoon–evening
· Day–night

Categorizing
· Straight–curved
· Round–circle; square–rectangle
· Line–dot
· Edge–side

Basic colors
· Problems in identifying differences, similarities

Size/Quantity
· Big–little
· Fast–slow
· Loud–soft
· Light–dark

OCULAR MOTOR CONTROL

Ocular motor control originates in the visual refractive reception system. The ocular-motor system consists of six coordinated pairs of eye muscles that function together to allow accurate vision of the environment. The two eyes coordinate as a team allowing incoming light to enter and to properly guide the body, particularly the limbs involved in coordinating movement. The major responsibility of ocular motor control is to fixate or track moving objects in space.

Basic Input Sensory Systems Involvement

KINESTHETIC

VISUAL

Checklist

· Inability to locate a particular object in space
· Difficulty in keeping place in reading
· Trouble tying shoe/shoe laces
· Difficulty in cutting, pasting
· Poor handwriting movements
· Inability to follow moving objects with eyes
· Inability to fixate eyes on objects
· Inability to make whole/part discrimination
· Can't tell the difference between like and unlike objects

BODY AWARENESS – "BODY IMAGE"

Body awareness involves how a person pictures their body, attitudes concerning their body, and their knowledge of their body's capabilities and limitations.

Because the body itself is the reference point, body awareness becomes the foundation for perceptual skills. Body image is the originator of the movement and a major factor in conception of himself as a person. The environmental contact and its interaction by the body is involved.

Basic Input Sensory Systems Involvement

ALL SYSTEMS

Checklist

· Does not know a body part or where it is located
· Bumps into objects
· Drops paper off desk
· Lacks balance skills
· May miss desk or chair when attempting to sit
· Difficulty in making quick changes in position
· Inability to identify body parts (own or in a picture)
· Difficulty in imitating a movement
· Under reaches (over reaches) an object
· Inaccurate estimation of body size relationship to objects/people

Functional Involvement

FUNCTIONAL ERRORS

Performance of Motor Skills

PHYSICAL FITNESS

Physical fitness centers around the concept of quality activity for the body. The accurate and appropriate activity for promoting physical development and fitness needs consideration. Health related fitness and performance related fitness are the two major aspects.

HEALTH RELATED FITNESS

Health related fitness includes those aspects that relate to physiological functioning that offer protection against disease through a proper life-style. Directed physical activity can improve and/or maintain this physical health and well-being in children. Components of the health related fitness are discussed as follows.

MUSCULAR STRENGTH
Muscular strength is the maximum amount of force exerted by a muscle. The strength of the muscle is dependent on its size and quality. Increase in muscle strength develops when there is an increase of resistance, duration of contraction (time is lengthened while maintaining constant resistance), or rate of muscle action. Running and bicycling increase leg strength while arm strength is increased through weight lifting, carrying large objects, or handling tools.

ENDURANCE
Endurance is the ability of a muscle to exert a force repeatedly over a particular time period. Static muscular endurance is to exert muscular force against resistance. Dynamic muscular endurance involves moving the resistance by force. Endurance involves the ability to work hard over a given time period and/or the ability to repeat identical movements or maintain a degree of tension over a given time frame. Activities involving a number of repetitions, such as sit-ups and push-ups, should be considered.

FLEXIBILITY
Flexibility is the capacity of a limb or body part to move throughout a range of motion. Flexibility is dependent on the flexibility/extensibility of ligaments and muscles surrounding the joints. Flexibility allows for freedom in movement. Bending, stretching, turning, and twisting are good activities to build flexible movement.

BODY COMPOSITION
Body composition relates to the relative percentage of fat to lean body mass. Body fat is the index of measurement of body weight. Consideration of both food intake as well as amount of exercise performed is involved. The consultation of medical personnel as to how to handle an overweight problem should be considered.

CARDIOVASCULAR FITNESS
Cardiovascular fitness is the ability of the heart, the blood vessels, and the respiratory system to deliver oxygen efficiently over a given period of time. The objective is to increase maximum amounts of oxygen that the body can process during a particular time period. Activities that are continuous and rhythmic, such as aerobics, walking, jumping rope, kicking, and swimming are important.

PERFORMANCE RELATED FITNESS

Performance-related fitness is referred to as one's motor fitness ability. The ability to perform several different skills is important. Children having good performance skills have athletic skill ability. Throwing, catching, climbing, and swimming are activities useful in developed motor fitness abilities. Components considered as motor fitness abilities are the following:

AGILITY
Agility is the ability to make a rapid change of body position in space with control. Included in such an ability is quick changes in direction, sudden stops, rapid starts, quick reactions, and finger dexterity. Agility can be developed through practice and confidence in movement. Activities involving such body movements include "up-down," "side-to-side," "forward-backward," swimming, and dodging.

SPEED
In moving from one point to another, the time taken divided by the distance is referred to as speed. It is influenced by reaction time and can be improved with practice. Good activities useful in developing speed include running and climbing. Various activities are available for the individual to increase speed but practice is the key.

BALANCE

Balance is a complex motor ability. Because it involves vision, inner ear, and neurological processing, it is detailed in the perceptual motor performance functioning section.

Incidental Involvement

SKILL COMPETENCIES
GROSS MOTOR SKILLS INVOLVEMENT

BASIC LOCOMOTION

Locomotion is a part of the performance related skills used to move the body from one place to another or to project the body upward. These movements are the foundation of gross motor coordination involving the large muscles and should be as purposeful and controlled as possible. Body mechanics, growth/developmental, and personal factors are involved to create accurate performance. These abilities are a necessary part of the individual's environment.

SKILL SEQUENCE

Step 1: Analyze the mechanics involved

Step 2: Decide on the basic patterns of movement needed to perform the skill

Step 3: Observe the individual's personal characteristics and emotional stability

Step 4: Be aware of the amount of balance/equilibrium that the individual controls when teaching the sequence

The suggested sequence for the locomotion skills to be taught is as follows:

SINGLE FUNDAMENTAL SKILLS

1. Running
2. Leaping
3. Jumping
4. Hopping

COMBINATION FUNDAMENTAL SKILLS

1. Skipping
2. Sliding
3. Galloping

SKILL COMPETENCIES
FINE MOTOR SKILLS INVOLVEMENT

Fine motor is the ability to control the small muscles of the body in expressive activity sequences. Development of the fine motor skills follows that of the gross motor skills. Development centers from the head to the toes and from the midline to the body extremities. In academic tasks these skills are involved with eye and hand control.

Fine motor involves simple manual dexterity and complex manual dexterity. Abilities involved in simple fine motor are aiming, reaction time involving dexterity, and fingers, and arm-hand, and wrist-finger performances. Complex fine motor abilities control activities relating to manual dexterity with response orientation to precision and rate control. Manual dexterity type activities include ability to grip (as a pencil), writing-cutting, and ocular pursuits involving teaching (join dots, sand tray, word cards).

SOURCES

Updated and detailed information is available through:

American Alliance for Health,
Physical Recreation, and Dance
1900 Association Drive
Reston VA 22091

Specific Learning Disability

A disorder in one or more of the basic psychological processes involved in understanding or in using language, spoken or written, which may manifest itself in an imperfect ability to listen, think, read, write, spell, or to do mathematical calculations. The term includes such conditions as perceptual handicaps, brain injury, minimal brain dysfunction, dyslexia, and developmental aphasia. The term does not include children who have learning problems which are primarily the result of visual, hearing, or motor handicaps, of mental retardation, of emotional disturbance, or of environmental, cultural, or economic disadvantage.

HANDWRITING

EXPRESSIVE PROBLEM

Handwriting is the functional support shell used in expressing language and communication. The major concerns include the ability to write legibly with ease and swiftness. Dysgraphia is the inability to write because of cerebral lesions.

The two major forms of handwriting used today are manuscript and cursive. Manuscript tends to require less fine motor control and eye movement coordination which is why it is introduced to young children as an expressive form of communication. Cursive is used formally in our society today and is more universal in the public domain.

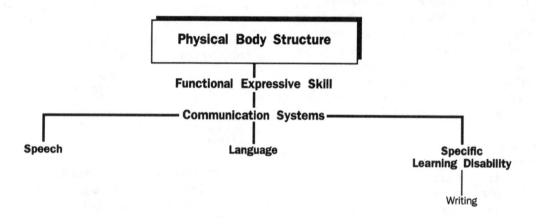

Vocabulary

Form: accurate formation of letters.

Size: uniform formation of letters on a given sheet of lined paper.

Line quality: measures evenness of writing pressure given by the instrument (light/heavy, thick/fine) writing.

Spacing: measurement of uniformity between letters in a word and word to word.

Alignment: the position of the written symbols as they are placed between the top and bottom line on a particular line. Do they "stay on the bottom or top of the line" of the paper?

Slant: a term used in cursive writing which denotes whether the slant is uniform and straight in relationship to better formation.

Left handed: a hand preference which requires adjustment to writing instructions taught.

Cursive writing: the uniform writing style used in most educational settings and in our American society.

Manuscript writing: an introductory form of teaching handwriting (printing) to children in the elementary school.

Checklist

Behaviors in Using Instrument
· Transfers objects from hand to hand
· Picks up small objects
· Strings large beads
· Holds writing implement properly
· Folds paper
· Can use scissors properly
· Writes neatly
· Formulates accurate letter forms
· Has difficulty in maintaining balance
· Falls off seat

Quality of Handwriting
· Formation of letters.
· Uniform size of the letters.
· Good spacing within words.
· Good spacing between sentences.
· Do letter/sentences maintain good positioning between the top and bottom of a given line?
· Is slant appropriate/uniform?
· Is there an evenness in the written word by the instrument being used?

· Is the written assignment neat?
· Are margins/indention of paragraphs accurate and uniform?

Fundamental Involvement

Fine motor skills are the key to development of handwriting skills. Muscles that relate to eye focusing on an image and finger dexterity often develop the major muscle groups that develop maturity. The growth patterns vary among children and fine muscle dexterity is often an influence when cursive handwriting skills should be taught. Experiences in finger painting, use of crayons, drawing, puzzles, and cutting/pasting type activities help in making decisions regarding the encouragement of the use of cursive handwriting techniques. Dysgraphia is a form of handwriting deficiency caused by a lesion to the brain and should be a consideration when cursive handwriting fails to develop.

Instruction in handwriting is encouraged throughout the elementary school program. As the child grows so do the skills required in producing legibility and improving accuracy.

Essential elements of legible handwriting are:

Letter formation: strokes used in both manuscript and cursive patterns. This involves slant, loops, and undercurve. Connecting of letters produced is important here.

Size and Proportion: a student's fine motor skills increase; letters decrease. Manuscript writing strokes transfer to cursive slant strokes.

Spacing: concern includes spacing between letters in words, between words and sentences so it is legible.

Slant: slant should be made in a consistent pattern with position of paper influencing the slant of the written word.

Alignment: letter size needs to be uniform in size and consistently touch the baseline of the paper.

Line quality: attention is given to consistent speed in formation of words and the holding of the instrument which influences consistent thickness in the writing process.

AGENCY/LEARNING DISABILITY

Association for Children and Adults with Learning Disabilities
4156 Library Road
Pittsburgh, PA 15234

Council for Learning Disabilities
P.O. Box 40303
Overland Park, KS 66204

National Center for Learning Disabled
99 Park Avenue, 6th Floor
New York, NY 10016

RELATED SERVICES

The All Handicapped Children's Act (AHCA) defines related services as "such developmental, corrective, and other supportive services . . . as may be required to assist a handicapped child to benefit from special education. Related services eligibility is based on the law that a child must be "handicapped" and special education is required. A "related service" must be necessary for a child to benefit from special education. A district's responsibility according to the Act was designed to maintain a "basic floor of opportunity." This floor consists of "access to specialized instruction and related services which are individually designed to provide educational benefit to the handicapped child."

Transportation

Transportation is included as a related service under Education of the Handicapped 20 U.S.C. 1404-1461. It is a part of a "free appropriate public education" assurance component stating that transportation must be provided at public expense, under public supervision and direction, and without charge. Its major purpose is to enable a child to be physically present in class.

Transportation must be provided if the district provides transportation for its general school population. Any school district which provides any special education program must provide transportation to any handicapped person qualifying for the particular special education institution or related service. When a school district does not provide transportation to its general school population it must decide on an individual basis whether transportation would benefit the special education of the handicapped individual.

Transportation includes services starting at the door of residence, to the vehicle, and to the special education and/or related service site or center. It may include to and from residential placement as well. Educational environments vary for the individuals having physical disabilities and health impairment in particular.

Transportation may entail these individuals going to hospital settings, self-contained classrooms, non-categorical special education classrooms, or regular education placement. Accessibility to the proper support services may cause modification problems in transportation. These responsibilities are important for the handicapped individual as well as the local educational agency involved and transportation responsibilities and delivery services are rendered by the education system involved.

Counseling/Psychological Services

A major component of related services involves both psychological and counseling assistance to handicapped individuals in special education. Public Law 94-142 defines psychological services as including:

"(I) Administering psychological and educational tests and other assessment procedures: (Native tongue required).

(II) Interpreting assessment results:

(III) Obtaining, integrating, and interpreting information about child behavior and conditions relating to learning:

(IV) Consulting with other staff members in planning school programs to meet the special needs of children as indicated by psychological tests, interviews, and behavioral evaluations: and

(V) Planning and managing a program of psychological services, including psychological counseling for children and parents."

Social Work Services in the schools is defined in Public Law 94-142 as including:
"(I) Preparing a social or development history on a handicapped child

(II) Group and individual counseling with the child and family

(III) Working with those problems in a child's living situation (home, school, and community) that affect the child's adjustment in school; and

(IV) Mobilizing school and community resources to enable the child to receive maximum benefit from his or her educational program."

Guidance services are a part of the general educa-

tion program that participates in the development of an educational plan for each handicapped individual requiring special education related services. The guidance counsellor is frequently the first person to make contact and is in a position to provide continual contact and services. Follow through of individual educational planning and monitoring that progress is often times the responsibility of the counselor.

SOURCES OF PROFESSIONAL HELP

Psychiatrist - A medical doctor specializing in psychiatry or applied behavior disorders.

Psychoanalyst - A medical doctor specializing in a particular field of psychiatry called psychotherapy under the influence of Freud.

Social Worker - Assesses social conditions, interviewing, assists rehabilitation into the community

Neurologist - Focuses on disorders of the nervous system that may influence behavior patterns.

Clinical Psychologist - Performs individual and group therapy sessions, assesses and diagnoses through formal testing procedures—both mental and emotional.

Guidance Counselor - Resides in an educational school site, usually in one building, assisting students who need guidance and counseling in that professional setting.

School Psychologist - Administers and interprets individual psychological and educational tests for gaining information pertinent to an individual educational plan.

Psychometrist - A trained professional in the administration and interpretation of academic achievement and behavioral tests.

Centers for Counseling/ Psychological Evaluation

Child guidance centers - A specialized center staffed with a cluster of trained professionals whose expertise centers around the needs of children.

Hospital psychiatric unit - Specialized areas in general hospital setting designated for intense psychological and counseling services.

Local mental health center - Public facility serving a certain community or designated area and providing services in counseling and psychological assistance. (Cost of services is pro-rated to the economy).

Play therapy - Used with children below the ages of eight, allowing through play to demonstrate how they feel about themselves and who is important in their lives at any designated center.

Group therapy - Interaction within a selected group of individuals to open up and expand communication; used in a designated counseling/psychological center.

Private hospitals - A private setting often centered around a particular philosophy used in treating individuals needing special care.

Psychotherapy - A process or treatment covering various kinds of counseling and guidance, individual, group, child, and family therapy and psychoanalysis.

Psychology - An educational approach studying human behavior using psychological and counseling techniques and procedures.

Medical/Health Services

Medical and health services are for diagnosis and evaluation purposes which help decide whether movement from regular educational programming to special education is essential. Before a child can enter special education a free physical examination from a medical doctor is required. Regulations require "related services" provisions including "school health services." School health services are provided by a qualified school nurse or other designated, qualified person. The service described in the law and its regulations must be reasonable to provide and pertinent to the educational process.

Health information compiled for each child referred to the ARC (Admissions and Release Committee) should contain a written description of medical, physical or pharmacological information which may affect educational performance. The following information may be found in such a report: motor functioning; medication used or on currently; a history of illness and accidents; need for medical assistance; medical limitations; chronic illness; history of drug and alcohol abuse; results of vision and hearing screening; trauma; emotional problems; and previous medical evaluations; services; and hospitalization.

MEDICAL/HEALTH PERSONNEL
School Nurse

The Rules of Special Education 12.17 (1) require a health history as part of the comprehensive evaluation.

Professional judgement regarding expanded health evaluations or reports related to potential or identified health problems is a major responsibility. When no health problem is present, a written report is filed into the child's folder. Attendance at individual educational program meetings is expected or information from such meetings should be given in written form to the school nurse. These are the major responsibilities of the school nurse as they relate to special education. The school nurse should assist the handicapped child by providing health care; assist the parents of handicapped children by acting as a liaison regarding health resource sites such as school, home, community; function as a health consultant and resource for school personnel.

Physical Therapist

The physical therapist organizes, develops, and implements a therapy program to minimize the effect of a physical disability or handicapping condition. The specific responsibilities of the physical therapist include: developing gross motor skill development; develop mobility (walking, crawling, wheelchair use, prosthetic devices); recommend equipment and training in the use of adaptive equipment (special chairs, leg braces, positioning equipment); consulting with and training staff in handling/positioning/safety of movements; development and monitoring respiratory functioning programs.

Occupational Therapist

The occupational therapist's role is to minimize the effect of a physical disability or handicapping condition by organizing, developing, and implementing a therapy program of an individual nature. The major roles and responsibilities of the occupational therapist include: a development of fine motor coordination; recommending equipment/training for a student to use in the classroom, for the individual himself, or his/her hand skills (dressing aids, eating aids, special chairs, prosthetic devices, splints); development of sensorimotor skills/sensory integration to classroom performances (motor planning, bilateral integration, tactile defensiveness); develop work simplifications and motor techniques for practical school usage.

School health services are varied from state to state and school district to school district. Many school districts provide little or no assistance in this area because of financial reasons. Health services remain a vital contributor to the special education program in the area of medical and physical facets of the total school program.

Medical Abbreviations

ā	before
abd	abdomen
a.c.	before meals
A.D.L.	activities of daily living
ad lib	as desired
amt.	amount
bid	twice a day
Bil	bilateral
BM	bowel movement
B.P.	blood pressure
c̄	with
cc	cubic centimeter
c/o	complains of
D.C.	discontinue
E	enema
emesis	vomitus
G-tube	gastrostomy tube
gavage	fed by N/G tube
GI	gastro-intestinal
gtts	drops
HC/EE	head circumference, ear to ear
H_2O	water
Kg	kilogram
L	left
lg	large
LOC	level of consciousness
mod	moderate
Na	sodium
N/G	naso-gastric tube
no	number
noc	night
N.P.O.	nothing by mouth
N/S	normal saline
OD	right eye
OS	left eye
OU	both eyes or each eye
oz	ounce
P̄	after
p.c.	after meals
per	through or by
p.o.	by mouth
p.r.n.	as necessary
q̄	every
q-d	every day
qid	four times a day
qod	every other day
R	right
REM	rapid eye movement
Resp.	respiratory
ROM	range of motion
s̄	without
s̄m	small
SOB	shortness of breath
stat	immediately

Temp	(po) orally
	(R) rectally
	(AX) axillary
tid	three times a day
trach	tracheostomy/tracheotomy
Vd	urinate
void	urinate
W/C	wheelchair
↓	down, less, decrease
↑	up, more, increase
#	pounds
>	more
<	less

Physical Body Structural Syatems

An emphasis on medically related services have a great influence on many types of handicapped individual whose physical body structure and motor systems are impaired. Both medical and technical assistance are required. Prescription drugs are used to help promote normal educational functioning. Detailed information concerning medications in the schools is found in Chapter 5 where special consideration is given to the severe emotionally disturbed handicapped.

Communication System

Specific communication problems relating to both speech and language may require special professional evaluation. A face evaluation must be given when an individual fails to function at a specific level. Technical assistance may be found through the following sources.

PROFESSIONAL PERSONNEL

Speech/language pathologist: evaluates, diagnoses, and remediates speech and language disorders relating to articulation, stuttering, voice, language learning disabilities; developmental apraxia and hearing impaired.
Orthodontist: a specialist who corrects occlusal abnormalities by surgery, repositioning segments of several teeth.
Plastic surgeon/pediatrician: a medical team used when assessment of orofacial defects are found (cleft lip/palate).

Devices

Speech and audiometry: a technique that tests a person's detection and understanding of speech.

Health Related

Specialized health needs may involve ventilator dependence, tracheostomy dependence, oxygen dependence, nutritional supplemental dependence, congestive heart problems, need long health term care, apnea monitoring and/or kidney dialysis.

PROFESSIONAL PERSONNEL

Medical Doctor (Specializing): a medically trained professional in the area of the body where impairment is located.
School Nurse: monitors medical directions that must be implemented in the educational setting.

AIDS

A child's participation in the school setting.is a basic health related problem. The Public Health Service recommends that under normal circumstances children with AIDS "should be allowed to attend school and after-school day care . . . ."

Things to remember:
1. AIDS is transmitted through direct exposure of a child's bloodstream to blood from an infected person.
2. Evaluation for special school placement should be similar to other children (eg. cerebral palsy).
3. Team decision needs to be made with medical personnel involved.
4. Most common symptoms among children is poor growth, enlargement of liver/spleen, Kapose's sarcoma (tumor of blood vessels occurring on skin surface).

Physical/Structural Motor Systems

Improvements in medical advances have assured the survival of more children with severe medical problems. Neurologically impaired and musculoskeletal conditions have increased causing the school to assume the responsibility of more related services in the medical area. Medical treatment for the physically disabled involves prosthetics, drug therapy, surgery, and rehabilitation. More and more technical services are being introduced in the school day as part of the educational plan for a handicapped individual.

PROFESSIONAL PERSONNEL

Orthopedist: a medical specialist who treats spine, form, and function of the extremities and associated structures through medical, surgical, and physical methods.
Neurologist: a medical specialist in the treatment of nervous diseases (neurosurgeon-specialized in operations on the nervous system).
Pharmacist: one who prepares and dispenses drugs and has knowledge concerning their properties.
Pharmacotherapist/chemotherapist: one who treats diseases by means of chemical substances or drugs.
Prosthetist: one skilled in constructing and fitting artificial parts of the human body. Prothesis - device that allows the person to do something - brace (orthosis).

AGENCY DIRECTORY

Information about a particular handicapping condition is often times not generally available. Parents, educators, health professionals, and everyone else who works with a particular identifiable handicap needs additional information about the handicap, services that are necessary and available, and the location of specified services. National organizations on specific disabilities or conditions focuses on information and support. Parent training and parent support groups offer general information, assistance, and support. Government agencies give information relating to laws and services. When help is needed there are many sources available to the handicapped person. When educational practices and general information appear sketchy and vague, help may be found through knowledgeable centers. These centers may be able to clarify the opportunities available to the handicapped person and a clearer route for the person directly involved with that individual who is handicapped.

Agency listings are given with addresses and telephone numbers when possible. Telephone numbers can, however, be obtained by dialing information in the city where the location is found. Do not give up if addresses are incorrect. Interagency information is available at any government center or clearing house. They are generally courteous and will assist the person when a need has been voiced to them.

The list of agencies used is largely found in a fact sheet distributed by NICHCY—The National Information Center for Children and Youth with Disabilities, P.O. Box 1492, Washington, D.C. 20013.

GOVERNMENT AGENCIES

Interprofessional Information

**Administration for Children,
Youth and Families**
P.O. Box 1182
Washington, D.C. 20013
(202) 245-0347

**Administration on Developmental
Disabilities (DHHS)**
329 D Humphrey Building
200 Independence Ave., S.W.
Washington, D.C. 20201
(202) 245-2890

**Bureau of Maternal and Child Health
and Resources Development**
Parklawn Building
5600 Fishers Lane
Rockville, MD 20857
(301) 443-2170

**District Internal Revenue
Service - Tax Information**
(800) 424-1040
(800) 424-FORM

**National Institute of Neurological &
Communicative Disorders**
NIH, Bldg. 31, Room 8A-06
Bethesda, MD 20892
(301) 496-4000

**National Library Service for the Blind
and Physically Handicapped**
Library of Congress
1291 Taylor Street, N.W.
Washington, D.C. 20542
(800) 424-8567

**Office of Disease Prevention
and Health Promotion**
National Health Information Center
P.O. Box 1133
Washington, D.C.
20013-1133, (800) 336-4797

**Department of Health and Human Services
(Medicare Information and
Second Surgical Opinion Program)**
Health Care Financing Administration
Baltimore, MD 21235

**National Center for Education
in Maternal and Child Health**
38th and R Streets, N.W.
Washington, D.C. 20625-8400

**National Information Center for
Children & Youth with Handicaps (NICHCY)**
P.O. Box 1492
Washington, D.C. 20013
(800) 999-5599
(703) 893-6061
(703) 893-8614 (TDD)

**National Institute of Child
Health and Human Development**
NIH, 9000 Rockville Pike
Bldg. 31, Room 2A03
Bethesda, MD 20892
(301) 496-3454

**President's Committee on Employment
of People with Disabilities**
1111 20th St., N.W., Suite 636
Washington, D.C. 20036-3470
(202) 653-5044
(202) 653-5050 (TDD)

**Public Information Office
National Library of Medicine**
Bethesda, MD 20894
(301) 496-4000

**Senate Subcommittee on
Disability Policy**
113 Hart Senate Office Bldg.
Washington, D.C. 20510
(202) 224-6265

Social Security Administration Hotline
(800) 234-5SSA
(800) 324-0778 (TDD)
(800) 392-0812 (in Mo./TDD)

**Office of Special Education
and Rehabilitation Services**
Clearinghouse on Disability Information
U.S. Dept. of Education
Room 3132, Switzer Bldg.,
330 C St., S.W.
Washington, D.C. 20202-2524
(202) 732-1723, (202) 732-1245

**Volunteers in Service to America
Foster Grandparent Program**
ACTION
Public Affairs Division
1100 Vermont Ave., N.W.
Washington, D.C. 20525

GENERAL INFORMATION

Public Agencies

STATE EDUCATION DEPARTMENT

The State Department staff can answer questions about special education and related services in your state. Many states have special manuals explaining the steps to take. Check to see if one is available. State Department officials are responsible for special education and related services programs in their state for preschool, elementary, and secondary age children.

STATE VOCATIONAL REHABILITATION AGENCY

The state vocational rehabilitation agency provides medical, therapeutics, counseling, education, training, and other services needed to prepare people with disabilities for work. This state agency will provide you with the address of the nearest rehabilitation office where you can discuss issues of eligibility and services with a counselor. The state vocational rehabilitation agency can also refer you to an independent living program in your state. Independent living programs provide services which enable adults with disabilities to live productively as members of their communities. The services might include, but are not limited to, information and referral, peer counseling, workshops, attendant care, and technical assistance.

OFFICE OF STATE COORDINATOR OF VOCATIONAL EDUCATION FOR HANDICAPPED STUDENTS

States receiving federal funds used for vocational education must assure that funding is used in programs which include students with handicaps. This office can tell you how your state funds are being used and provide you with information on current programs.

STATE MENTAL RETARDATION/DEVELOPMENTAL DISABILITIES AGENCIES

The functions of state mental retardation/developmental disabilities agencies vary from state to state. The general purpose of this office is to plan, administer and develop standards for state/local mental retardation/developmental disabilities programs provided in state-operated facilities and community-based programs. This office provides information about available services to families, consumers, educators and professionals.

STATE DEVELOPMENTAL DISABILITIES COUNCIL

Assisted by the U.S. Department of Health and Human Services' Administration on Developmental Disabilities, state councils plan and advocate for improvement in services for people with developmental disabilities. In addition, funding is made available for time-limited demonstration and stimulatory grant projects.

STATE MENTAL HEALTH AGENCIES

The functions of state mental health agencies vary from state to state. The general purposes of these offices are to plan, administer, and develop standards for state and local mental health programs such as state hospitals and community health centers. They can provide information to the consumer about mental illness and a resource list of contacts where you can go for help.

PROTECTION AND ADVOCACY AGENCY AND CLIENT ASSISTANCE PROGRAM

Protection and advocacy systems are responsible for pursuing legal, administrative and other remedies to protect the rights of people who are developmentally disabled or mentally ill, regardless of their age. Protection and advocacy agencies may provide information about health, residential, and social service in your are. Legal assistance is also available.

The Client Assistance Program provides assistance to individuals seeking and receiving vocational rehabilitation services. These services, provided under the Rehabilitation Act of 1973, include assisting in the pursuit of legal, administrative, and other appropriate remedies to ensure the protection of the rights of individuals with developmental disabilities.

PROGRAMS FOR CHILDREN WITH SPECIAL HEALTH CARE NEEDS

The U.S. Department of Health and Human Services' Office of Maternal and Child Health and Resource Development provides grants to states for direct medical and related services to children with handicapping conditions. Although services will vary from state to state, additional programs may be funded for retraining, research, special projects, genetic disease testing, and counseling services. For additional information about current grants and programs in your state, contact:

**National Center for Education
in Maternal and Child Health**
38th and R Streets, NW
Washington, D.C. 20057.

UNIVERSITY AFFILIATED PROGRAMS

A national network of programs affiliated with universities and teaching hospitals, UAPs provides interdisciplinary training for professionals and paraprofessionals and offers programs and services for children with disabilities and their families. Some UAPs provide direct services for children and families. Individual UAPs have staff with expertise in a variety of areas and can provide information, technical assistance, and inservice training to agencies, service providers, parent groups, and others.

A listing of all University Affiliated Programs may be obtained by contacting:

The Maternal and Child Health Clearing House
38th and R Streets, N.W.
Washington, D.C. 20057.

DISABILITY AGENCIES

ALLERGIES & ASTHMA

**Asthma and Allergy
   Foundation of America**
1717 Massachusetts Ave., N.W.
Suite 305
Washington, D.C. 20036

AMPUTATION

National Amputation Foundation
12-45 150th Street
Whitestone, N.Y. 11357

ARTHRITIS

American Juvenile Arthritis Organization
Arthritis Foundation
1314 Spring Street, N.W.
Atlanta, GA 30309

ATAXIA

Friedreich's Ataxia Group in America, Inc.
P.O. Box 11116
Oakland, CA 94611

National Ataxia Foundation
600 Twelve Oaks Center
15500 Wayzata Boulevard
Wayzata, MN 55391

AUTISM

Autism Society of America
8601 Georgia Ave., Suite 503
Silver Spring, MD 20910

BRAIN TUMOR

Association for Brain Tumor Research
3725 N. Talman
Chicago, IL 60618

CANCER

American Cancer Society
1499 Clifton Road, N.E.
Atlanta, GA 30329

CEREBRAL PALSY

United Cerebral Palsy Assoc.
7 Penn Plaza, Suite 804
New York, NY 10001

CLEFT PALATE

National Cleft Palate Assoc.
1218 Grandview
Pittsburgh, PA 15211

Prescription Parents, Inc.
P.O. Box 161
W. Roxbury, MA 02132

CRI DU CHAT (CAT CRY SYNDROME)

The 5p- Society
11609 Oakmont
Overland Park, KS 66210

CYSTIC FIBROSIS

Cystic Fibrosis Foundation
6931 Arlington Road
Bethesda, MD 20814

DIABETES

Juvenile Diabetes Foundation International
432 Park Avenue, South
New York, NY 10016

EPILEPSY

Epilepsy Foundation of America (EFA)
4351 Garden City Drive
Landover, MD 20785

FACIAL

**National Assoc. for the
Craniofacially Handicapped**
P.O. Box 11082
Chattanooga, TN 37401

HEMOPHILIA

National Hemophilia Foundation
110 Green St Room 406
New York NY 10012

Canadian Hemophilia Society
1450 City Councillors, Ste. 840
Montreal, Quebec
Canada, H3A 2E6

HEART DISORDERS

American Heart Association
7320 Greenville Avenue
Dallas, TX 75231

National Kidney Foundation
30 East 33rd Street, 11th floor
New York, NY 10016

LIVER DISORDERS

Children's Liver Foundation, Inc.
1425 Ventura Boulevard
Suite 201
Sherman Oaks, CA 91423

LUNG DISEASES

American Lung Association
1740 Broadway
New York, NY 10019

MUSCULAR DYSTROPHY

Muscular Dystrophy Association
810 Seventh Avenue
New York, NY 10019

ORTHOPEDIC AND BURN PROBLEMS

International Shriners Headquarters
Shriners Hospitals for Crippled Children
2900 Rocky Point Drive
Tampa, FL 33607

RETT SYNDROME

**International Rett
Syndrome Association**
8511 Rose Marie Drive
Fort Washington, MD 20744

REYE'S SYNDROME

National Reye's Syndrome Foundation
P.O. Box 829
Bryan, OH 43506

SEIZURE DISORDER

**Intractable Seizure Disorder
Support Group**
c/o Barbara Schwan
29 Melrose Terrace
Middletown, NJ 07748

SICKLE CELL DISEASE

**National Association for Sickle
Cell Disease, Inc. (NASCD)**
3345 Wilshire Boulevard, Ste 1106
Los Angeles CA 90010-1880

SPINA BIFIDA

Spina Bifida Association of America
1700 Rockville Pike, Suite 250
Rockville, MD 20852-1654

SPINAL CORD INJURIES

**National Spinal Cord
Injury Association**
600 W. Cummings Pk., #2000
Woburn, MA 01801

STUTTERING

National Center for Stuttering
200 E. 33rd Street
New York, NY 10016

Speech Foundation of America
P.O. Box 11749
Memphis, TN 38111-0749

TAY-SACHS DISEASE

**National Tay-Sachs and Allied
   Diseases Association**
385 Elliot Street
Newton, MA 02164

TOURETTE SYNDROME

Tourette Syndrome Association
42-40 Bell Boulevard
Bayside, NY 11361-2861

CHAPTER 5

Manifestation #4 – Behavior Deviation

SERIOUSLY EMOTIONALLY DISTURBED

The definition of Seriously Emotionally Disturbed, according to PL-142, is stated as follows:

"(I.) A condition exhibiting one or more of the following characteristics over a long period of time and to a marked degree, which adversely affects educational performance: (A) an inability to learn which cannot be explained by intellectual, sensory or health factors; (B) an inability to build or maintain satisfactory interpersonal relationships with peers and teachers; (C) inappropriate types of behavior or feelings under normal circumstances; (D) a general pervasive mood of unhappiness or depression; or (E) a tendency to develop physical symptoms or fears associated with personal or school problems. (II) The term includes children who are schizophrenic. The term does not include children who are socially maladjusted, unless it is determined that they are seriously emotionally disturbed.

Under these conditions, money and services are available through federal government guidelines. Any child that meets these guidelines is eligible and cannot be refused!

It is a recognized fact that major learning disabilities supported under the federal law PL 94-142 are often accompanied by emotional problems arising from their inability to cope with any major handicap. This is called a secondary emotional problem. As positive adjustment develops to the handicap, the emotional problems or reactions tend to disappear. PL 94-142 separates this type of manifestation from the *Seriously Emotionally Disturbed*.

Consideration is given to a category whose primary problem is diagnosed as being *Seriously Emotionally Disturbed*. The category is characterized with behavior manifestations dealing largely with interpersonal relationships. This makes it a part of the expressive delivery system. The origin of this problem is under a great deal of scrutiny. We must be aware of the physical malfunctions that could occur in the various systems of the body (nervous, circulatory, glandular, etc.) which may be a direct influence on the expressive delivery system and result in inappropriate interpersonal relationships.

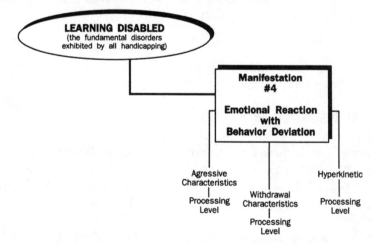

Physical Structure for All Individuals Suffering with Handicapping Characteristics

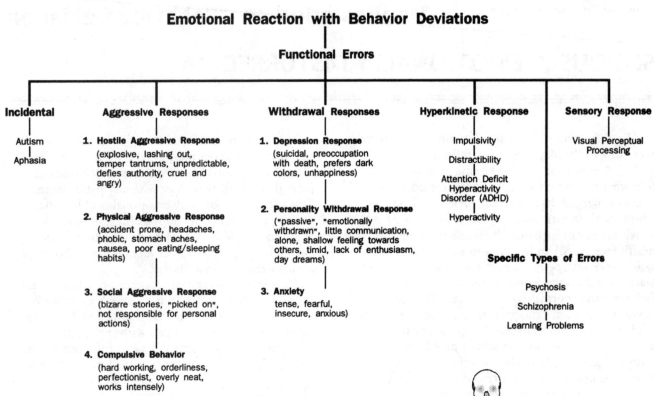

Emotional Reaction with Behavior Deviations

Functional Errors

Incidental

Autism

Aphasia

Aggressive Responses

1. **Hostile Aggressive Response**
   (explosive, lashing out, temper tantrums, unpredictable, defies authority, cruel and angry)

2. **Physical Aggressive Response**
   (accident prone, headaches, phobic, stomach aches, nausea, poor eating/sleeping habits)

3. **Social Aggressive Response**
   (bizarre stories, "picked on", not responsible for personal actions)

4. **Compulsive Behavior**
   (hard working, orderliness, perfectionist, overly neat, works intensely)

Withdrawal Responses

1. **Depression Response**
   (suicidal, preoccupation with death, prefers dark colors, unhappiness)

2. **Personality Withdrawal Response**
   ("passive", "emotionally withdrawn", little communication, alone, shallow feeling towards others, timid, lack of enthusiasm, day dreams)

3. **Anxiety**
   tense, fearful, insecure, anxious)

Hyperkinetic Response

Impulsivity

Distractibility

Attention Deficit Hyperactivity Disorder (ADHD)

Hyperactivity

Sensory Response

Visual Perceptual Processing

Specific Types of Errors

Psychosis

Schizophrenia

Learning Problems

Specific Seriously Emotionally Disturbed Functionally Disturbed Characteristics and Behaviors

HYPERACTIVITY
excessive or abnormal energy and/or activity level of functioning which interferes with normal learning situations. It may be called attention deficit disorder.

HYPERKINETIC
a medical term describing excessive motor activity; characterized as hyperactive or distractable.

ATTENTION DEFICIT DISORDER (WITH HYPERACTIVITY)
assessed before the age of 7 with characteristics including inattention, aggression, conduct disorders, and impulsivity. It may be called hyperactivity.

DISTRACTIBILITY
a tendency to be easily drawn to extraneous stimuli, an inability to focus on unimportant details, generally considered as a behavior response of the central nervous system.

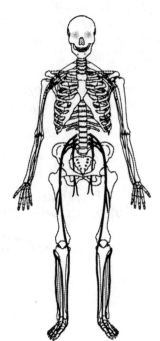

PERSEVERATION
tendency to continue a response beyond the normal end point of behavior, tendency to have difficulty in changing tasks.

SHORT ATTENTION SPAN
an inability to adequately devote the time to move a task toward completion without attending to something else.

EMOTIONAL LIABILITY

an ambivalent condition in which an individual display unstable moods by exhibiting rapid shifts from one extreme to another.

IMPULSIVITY

an abrupt response given with no regard to consequences or circumstances.

FRUSTRATION

an affective state where an individual cannot satisfy a particular need or goal.

SELF-CONTROL

a socially acceptable manner for a given individual to direct his own activity(s).

INTERPERSONAL PROBLEMS

inability to maintain satisfactory relationships with peers and teachers.

INTERPERSONAL RELATIONSHIPS

a general and pervasive mood of unhappiness or depression, a tendency to develop physical symptoms or fears associated with personal or school problems.

CIRCUMSTANTIAL/SITUATIONAL INAPPROPRIATENESS

inappropriate types or feelings under normal settings and/or circumstances.

SPECIFIC EMOTIONALLY DISTURBED REACTIONS

Aggressive Characteristics

A disruptive behavior consistently found with formal emotionally disturbed reactions is aggression. Aggression may be defined as an action carried out forcefully. Aggressive reactions may take on the form of physical or verbal abuse. A person who performs a physical action against himself or harms or creates fear against others is considered using physical aggression. Such self-destructive activities include hitting, scratching to throwing oneself against a hard object.

Verbal aggression takes on the form of non-physical or hostile action against oneself or others. It is characterized by self-destructive remarks. The goal appears to be to inflict psychological damage on oneself.

Withdrawal Characteristics

The child exhibiting severe emotional disturbances tends to react with extreme behavior patterns. The opposite of aggressive behavior is withdrawing patterns favoring escaping or leaving a particular life situation. The behavior takes on the form of isolation, fear, shyness, anxiety, depression, and day dreaming.

Hyperkinetic Characteristics

Hyperkinesis is a general term that encompasses such behavior terminology as hyperactivity, overactivity, and attention deficit disorder (ADD). Hyperkinesis, medically speaking, is defined as an excessive motor activity. Hyperactive children overact or over react to stimuli in their environment. Their behavior is characterized by fidgeting, restlessness, impulsiveness, and quarrelsomeness. Educationally, classroom teachers complain about self-control, short attention span, distractibility, and a low frustration or tolerance level of functioning.

Checklist

Aggression Responses
- Disobedience
- Disruptiveness
- Fighting
- Jealousy
- Bossiness
- Attention Seeking
- Boisterousness
- Quarrelsome
- Profanity
- Assaultiveness
- Clumsiness
- Stealing
- Signs of anger
- Habitually truant from school
- Stays out late at night
- Head Banging
- Has bad companions
- Strong alliance to certain peers

Withdrawal Responses
- Irritability
- Self-consciousness
- Social withdrawal
- Shyness
- Anxiety
- Seldom smiles
- Depression, chronic sadness

- Sensitive
- Seclusive
- Sluggish
- Crying
- Passive
- Daydreaming
- Jealousy
- Chews fingernails
- Drowsiness
- Prefers younger
    playmates
- Picked on by others
- Feelings of inferiority
- Inadequate guilt
    feelings

Hyperactivity Responses
- Fighting
- Temper tantrums
- Irresponsibility
- Boisterousness
- Irritability
- Crying
- Chews fingernails
- Short attention span
- Giggles
- Easily flustered
- Profanity
- Preoccupation
- Clumsiness
- Chews objects
- Unable to cope
- Fidgety
- Restlessness
- Impulsiveness
- Quarrelsome
- Overactive

Seriously Emotionally Disturbed

Incidental Involvement

INCIDENTAL ERRORS

AUTISM

Autism is a severely incapacitating developmental disability that usually appears during the first three years of life (definition by Autism Society of America). The symptoms of autism are a conglomeration of several handicaps. It is primarily a two-way social interaction and communication disorder. The communication problems contribute to irregular behavior patterns. Autism is considered by federal law classification as primarily a communication disorder and is further explained in that section.

APHASIA

Aphasia is a technical name given for interference with the comprehension and use of language—a condition which can follow injury to the brain (American Heart Association). Aphasia develops from conditions where brain damage is present. It is sometimes characterized as living in a world of "scrambled" communication.

Behavior changes take place frequently after injury occurs. Frequent characteristic behavior manifestations include low levels of frustration tolerance, self-centered, irritability, acts impulsively, and is prone to extreme mood changes. Further information concerning aphasia is under communication disorders.

Functional Involvement

FUNCTIONAL ERRORS

AGGRESSIVE RESPONSES

Acting out behavior which continues over a long period of time is classified as a serious emotional disturbance. Such behavior involves actions which may result in either physical or psychological injury to another individual. Acts included in such physical manifestations are kicking, hitting to physical fighting, and verbal abuses such as making threats, shouting insults, to the actual destruction of another's property. Their behavior signals an inappropriate coping with their environment. This manifestation is listed as aggressive responses and those children who produce such behaviors are considered as seriously emotionally disturbed. Aggressive or acting out types of behavior which continue over a long period and signal an inability to cope with the environment around them are:

1. Aggressive responses producing hostile situations.

2. Aggressive responses producing physically harmful situations.

3. Aggressive responses producing socially inappropriate behaviors.

4. Aggressive responses producing compulsive behavior patterns.

Hostility may present itself as a negative emotional behavior in certain children. The individual exhibits anger towards individuals and/or objects that are a part of his/her environment involving problems or discomfort. Major symptoms characterizing such behavior include: (1) blaming others for his/her problems; (2) suspicious of people he/she directly interacts with; (3) expresses a disdainful attitude. The individual him/herself appears bitter and resentful.

Personality characteristics include:

- explosive
- unpredictable
- cruel
- irritable
- fault-finding
- lashing out
- defies authority
- angry
- complaining
- resentful

Physical manifestations may result in aggressive behavior. The aggressive behavior is directed internally rather than towards his/her immediate environment. Major symptoms characterizing such behaviors include: (1) obvious physical injury, (2) physical complaints, (3) poor health habits.

Personality characteristics include:

- accident prone
- phobias
- poor eating habits
- poor sleeping habits
- headaches
- stomach aches
- nausea
- vomiting

Social aggressive responses may contribute to behavior of an extreme nature lasting over an extended period of time. The individual's interaction as a social being is involved. Basic symptoms involve (1) failure to meet social demands required of him/her, (2) inappropriate personal reactions, (3) exaggerated personal responses.

- Personality characteristics include:
- Bizarre stories
- "Picked on" (tattling)
- Failure to take responsibility for actions performed
- Untruthfulness

Compulsive behavior is considered as having aggressive traits which involved the personality of the person. Although outward appearances make this behavioral disturbance less offensive, inwardly it is extremely serious for the individual him/herself.

Symptomologically, the child appears (1) intense and hard working and (2) having excessive orderliness and conscientiousness.

Personality characteristics often associated with such excessive behaviors include:

- intensity
- hard working
- cleanliness
- conscientious
- orderly
- capacity for large amounts of work

Although aggressive manifestations may be easily identified, it may be difficult to prove clinically. Our general society promotes extreme aggressive acts as acceptable and positive. Acts of violence and aggressiveness are merely a turn of the knob away for every individual in our society. It is becoming increasingly more difficult to realize what is acceptable and unacceptable aggressive behavior, especially for individuals who are prone to aggressive behaviors and actions.

WITHDRAWAL RESPONSES

Withdrawal manifestations are characteristics of the emotionally disturbed internalizing their behavior over extended time periods. Fundamentally, individuals who respond in such a manner fail to initiate interaction with others; retreat from situations involving social interaction, and show excessive anxiety or fear behaviors. Identification of such responses is often passed over by professionals directly involved with diagnosis. However, they remain extremely serious and need professional diagnosis and help.

Withdrawal types of behavior which require diagnosis and modified educational programming are:

(1) Internalizing behavior revolving around depression.

(2) Personality withdrawal from everyday social-type situations (passive-emotionally withdrawn).

(3) Anxiety/fear extreme behaviors.

Depression is considered a mood disorder. Children's moods tend to have rapid change patterns. When the lowering of the mood (withdrawal) is persistent, and reduces the child's daily activities, we refer to it as depression or melancholy. In children, this generally is an environmental problem often resulting from the loss of a loved one, particularly the mother. The end result is a withdrawal type behavior resulting in failure to respond to their immediate environment.

Personality characteristics often associated with mood changes leading to depression are:

- anxiety
- refusal to go to school
- excessive sleep patterns
- preoccupation with death
- suicide tendencies
- unhappiness
- prefers dark colors
- headaches, stomach pains

PERSONALITY WITHDRAWAL RESPONSES
"PASSIVE" – "EMOTIONALLY WITHDRAWN"

Personality responses are dependent upon a person's emotional, mental, and temperamental make-up. Passive or emotionally withdrawn behaviors are influenced by the individual's actions and reactions to his/her peers and adults. Symptoms influencing such personality problems involve: (1) uncertainty of the correct response required, (2) inability to perform a correct response, (3) inability to comprehend a social situation involving two or more people, (4) responses are performed pathologically because of fear, insecurity, or frustration.

Personality characteristics involving personality withdrawal type behaviors which may be exhibited:

- lack of communication
- a loner
- shallow feelings towards others
- lack of enthusiasm
- anger bottled up
- timid
- submissive
- day dreamer
- reverts to fantasy behavior

ANXIETY

Anxiety may be defined as an internal signal system manifesting a distressed or apprehensive state. Anxiety involves things that are wrong, overwhelming, or unexpected. Individuals exhibiting anxiety-withdrawal characteristics tend to show "too little" behavior characteristics. They reflect their behavior through feeling states or bodily states. Some of these characteristics are as follows:

Feeling States	Body States
apprehensive	chest pains
dread	dizziness
fearful	headaches
overconcerned	nausea
restless	sweating
tense	weakness
worried	tiredness

HYPERKINETIC RESPONSES

"HYPERACTIVITY" - ATTENTION DEFICIT DISORDER (ADD)

Hyperkinesis is a condition where a high degree of physical activity is exhibited by the individual. This activity is excessive, and often leads to significantly impaired attention spans. Childhood vitality should not be confused with this problem but rather one must consider whether the excessive overactivity is appropriate or inappropriate behavior.

Hyperkinetic types of responses which require individual consideration when dealing with this kind of behavior manifestation are:

(1) impulsivity
(2) distractibility
(3) attention-deficit hyperactivity disorder (ADHD)

Impulsivity is the tendency to act hastily prior to the consideration of the consequences of the act. Built up energy seems to spill out at the least provocation. This particularly hinders a child in learning where problem solving is required. This child tends to be off and running before an assignment has been given.

Distractibility involves the inability to focus on important details. The individual is often drawn to extraneous stimuli which hampers the process of learning. An inability to focus in a structured manner leads to irrelevant and bizarre responses to relatively a easy curriculum.

Attention-deficit hyperactivity disorder (ADHD) address the issue of the recent prominence of attention problems interfering with the learning process. ADHD, a term suggested by the American Psychiatric Association, focuses on problems revolving around immaturity, excessive motor activity, and inappropriate processing in thinking. Symptoms include poor concentration, sluggish type behavior, and, of course, a very short attention span.

Hyperactivity is a dysfunction of, or delay in, the central nervous system involving exaggerated responses which interrupt the learning process. It is used synonymously with ADHD and hyperkinesis. Symptoms include: fidgeting, low frustration tolerance, inordinate movements, hard to manage, irritable, and quick shifts in moods. These signals are evident early in life.

Characteristics established as manifestations of hyperkinesis include:

- overactivity
- restlessness
- irritability
- underachievement
- clumsy
- undisciplined
- low frustration level
- quarrels with peers
- inattentive
- poor sleeper

PERCEPTUAL DISTORTIONS

Perceptually impaired individuals experience a limitation in reception of, integration of, or an effective response to sensory information. The basic problem centers around an inability to interpret a stimulation transmitted by a given sensory organ. This includes the sensory processes of eyes, ears, taste, smell, touch, and movement. Emotionally disturbed people may exhibit limitations in sensory receptors leading to the brain. This is particularly true in cross-modality perception the neurological process of converting information received through one receptive sensory modality to another system within the brain. Cross-modality may be labeled as transduction, intersensory integration, intermodal transfer. With the emotionally disturbed the process is considered more of a distortion rather than interpretation. Example: an individual may see visions or have false perceptions of taste, smell, or touch.

Incidental Involvement

SPECIFIC TYPES OF ERRORS

Psychosis

Psychosis is a disorder of the mental processes. When the daily demands of life are no longer functioning, we place them under this clinical psychological category. An additional impairment includes an inability to or distortion of reality. Children with psychotic tendencies have disorganized thinking, extreme mood variation patterns, fantasies, and withdrawal from the world of reality.

Schizophrenia

A type of psychosis manifesting itself in the behavior of certain young children is clinically labeled childhood schizophrenia. Onset is sometimes found as early as five years of age although frequently it makes its appearance in early adolescence. Possible symptoms associated with this particular pattern of behavior include extreme mood variations, poor concept formation, poor intellectual functioning, and an inability to interpret the world of reality.

RELATED SERVICES

The All Handicapped Children's Act (AHCA) defines related services as "such developmental, corrective, and other supportive services . . . as may be required to assist a handicapped child to benefit from special education. Related services eligibility is based on the law that a child must be "handicapped" and special education is required. A "related service" must be necessary for a child to benefit from special education. A district's responsibility according to the Act was designed to maintain a "basic floor of opportunity." This floor consists of "access to specialized instruction and related services which are individually designed to provide educational benefit to the handicapped child."

Transportation

Transportation is included as a related service under Education of the Handicapped 20 U.S.C. 1404-1461. It is a part of a "free appropriate public education" assurance component stating that transportation must be provided at public expense, under public supervision and direction, and without charge. Its major purpose is to enable a child to be physically present in class.

Transportation must be provided if the district provides transportation for its general school population. Any school district which provides any special education program must provide transportation to any handicapped person qualifying for the particular special education institution or related service. When a school district does not provide transportation to its general school population it must decide on an individual basis whether the transportation would benefit the special education of the handicapped individual.

Transportation includes service starting at the door of the residence, to the vehicle, and to the special education and/or related service site or center. It may include to and from residential placement as well. Special public and private institutions which provide specialized services for specific types of clinical classifications may qualify for transportation arrangements made by the school system.

Negotiating these arrangements is dependent upon the special education services offered by the district and upon which setting is most beneficial for the educational growth of the particular individual involved. Automatic placement into the school system's provisions is not necessarily in the best interests of the handicapped individual.

Counseling/Psychological Services

A major component of related services involves both psychological and counseling assistance to handicapped individuals in special education. Public Law 94-142 defines psychological services as including:

"(I) Administering psychological and educational tests and other assessment procedures: (native tongue required);

(II) Interpreting assessment results;

(III) Obtaining, integrating, and interpreting information about child behavior and conditions relating to learning;

(IV) Consulting with other staff members in planning school programs to meet the special needs of children as indicated by psychological tests, interviews, and behavioral evaluations; and

(V) Planning and managing a program of psychological services, including psychological counseling for children and parents."

Social Work Services in the schools is defined in Public Law 94-142 as including:
"(I) Preparing a social or development history on a handicapped child;

(II) Group and individual counseling with the child and family;

(III) Working with those problems in a child's living situation (home, school, and community) that affect the child's adjustment in school; and

(IV) Mobilizing school and community resources to enable the child to receive maximum benefit from his or her educational program."

Guidance services are a part of the general education program that participates in the development of an educational plan for each handicapped individual requiring special education related services. The guidance counsellor is frequently the first person to make contact and is in a position to provide continual contact and services. Follow through of individual educational planning and monitoring that progress is often times the responsibility of the counselor.

SOURCES OF PROFESSIONAL HELP

Psychiatrist - A medical doctor specializing in psychiatry or applied behavior disorders.

Psychoanalyst - A medical doctor specializing in a particular field of psychiatry called psychotherapy under the influence of Freud.

Social Worker - Assesses social conditions, interviewing, assists rehabilitation into the community

Neurologist - Focuses on disorders of the nervous system that may influence behavior patterns.

Clinical Psychologist - Performs individual and group therapy sessions, assesses and diagnoses through formal testing procedures—both mental and emotional.

Guidance Counselor - Resides in an educational school site, usually in one building, assisting students who need guidance and counseling in that professional setting.

School Psychologist - Administers and interprets individual psychological and educational tests for gaining information pertinent to an individual educational plan.

Psychometrist - A trained professional in the administration and interpretation of academic achievement and behavioral tests.

Centers for Counseling/ Psychological Evaluation

Child guidance centers - A specialized center staffed with a cluster of trained professionals whose expertise centers around the needs of children.

Hospital psychiatric unit - Specialized areas in general hospital setting designated for intense psychological and counseling services.

Local mental health center - Public facility serving a certain community or designated area and providing services in counseling and psychological assistance. (Cost of services is pro-rated to the economy).

Play therapy - Used with children below the ages of eight, allowing through play to demonstrate how they feel about themselves and who is important in their lives at any designated center.

Group therapy - Interaction within a selected group of individuals to open up and expand communication; used in a designated counseling/psychological center.

Private hospitals - A private setting often centered around a particular philosophy used in treating individuals needing special care.

Psychotherapy - A process or treatment covering various kinds of counseling and guidance, individual, group, child, and family therapy and psychoanalysis.

Psychology - An educational approach studying human behavior using psychological and counseling techniques and procedures.

Medical/Health Services
Medical and health services are for diagnosis and evaluation purposes which help decide whether movement from regular educational programming to special education is essential. Before a child can enter special education a free physical examination from a medical doctor is required. Regulations require

"related services" provisions including "school health services." School health services are provided by a qualified school nurse or other designated, qualified person. The service described in the law and its regulations must be reasonable to provide and pertinent to the educational process.

Health information compiled for each child referred to the ARC (Admissions and Release Committee) should contain a written description of medical, physical or pharmacological information which may affect educational performance. The following information may be found in such a report: motor functioning; medication used or on currently; a history of illness and accidents; need for medical assistance; medical limitations; chronic illness; history of drug and alcohol abuse; results of vision and hearing screening; trauma; emotional problems; and previous medical evaluations; services; and hospitalization.

MEDICAL/HEALTH PERSONNEL

School Nurse

The Rules of Special Education 12.17 (1) require a health history as part of the comprehensive evaluation. Professional judgement regarding expanded health evaluations or reports related to potential or identified health problems is a major responsibility. When no health problem is present, a written report is filed into the child's folder. Attendance at individual educational program meetings is expected or information from such meetings should be given in written form to the school nurse. These are the major responsibilities of the school nurse as they relate to special education. The school nurse should assist the handicapped child by providing health care; assist the parents of handicapped children by acting as a liaison regarding health resource sites such as school, home, community; function as a health consultant and resource for school personnel.

Physical Therapist

The physical therapist organizes, develops, and implements a therapy program to minimize the effect of a physical disability or handicapping condition. The specific responsibilities of the physical therapist include: developing gross motor skill development; develop mobility (walking, crawling, wheelchair use, prosthetic devices); recommend equipment and training in the use of adaptive equipment (special chairs, leg braces, positioning equipment); consulting with and training staff in handling/positioning/safety of movements; development and monitoring respiratory functioning programs.

Occupational Therapist

The occupational therapist's role is to minimize the effect of a physical disability or handicapping condition by organizing, developing, and implementing a therapy program of an individual nature. The major roles and responsibilities of the occupational therapist include: a development of fine motor coordination; recommending equipment/training for a student to use in the classroom, for the individual himself, or his/her hand skills (dressing aids, eating aids, special chairs, prosthetic devices, splints); development of sensorimotor skills/sensory integration to classroom performances (motor planning, bilateral integration, tactile defensiveness); develop work simplifications and motor techniques for practical school usage.

School health services are varied from state to state and school district to school district. Many school districts provide little or no assistance in this area because of financial reasons. Health services remain a vital contributor to the special education program in the area of medical and physical facets of the total school program.

EMOTIONAL REACTIONS WITH BEHAVIOR DEVIATION

Medical services may be involved with seriously emotionally disturbed when intake of drugs, prescribed by professional personnel (psychiatrists, etc.), is required during school hours.

Many medical services personnel, especially the school nurse, will also encounter problems where psychological factors will affect a physical condition. This condition may be described as "psychosomatic" or "psychophysiological."

Medication may need to be administered when that prescribed medication's intake is required during school hours. Certain procedures need to be followed under such conditions. A written permission is necessary for the school to participate in the prescribed procedure. Medication must be placed in a safe, designated location such as the principal's office or the school nurse's office. The container received by the school must be appropriately labeled by the pharmacist or physician. Sample medication and over-the-counter drugs need doctor's statements for permission. Those administering the drugs need a firm knowledge of the side effects of the medication. Recording of the date, time, and signature of the person giving the drug on the designated Medication Record is extremely important. Storage of the medication should be in a locked cabinet.

Seriously emotionally disturbed individuals will manifest their behavior deviances through physical conditions. The medical personnel will find themselves involved with individuals whose symptoms are gastrointestinal, pain oriented, or sexually based. These symptoms may be described as follows:

GASTROINTESTINAL SYMPTOMS:
1. Vomiting
2. Nausea
3. Diarrhea
4. Food intolerance

PAIN SYMPTOMS:
1. Headache
2. Backache
3. Dizziness
4. Shortness of breath

SEXUAL SYMPTOMS AFFECTED:
1. Burning sensation during urination
2. Sexual indifference
3. Painful menstruation
4. Excessive bleeding during menstruation

When the above symptoms persist, medical service personnel who are centered in the school setting should make recommendations for psychological/counseling assistance.

PROFESSIONAL PERSONNEL

Medical doctor (specializing): A medically trained professional in the area of the body where symptoms of gastrointestinal, pain, or sexual nature are exhibited.

School nurse: Monitors medical directions that must be implemented within the educational setting.

Neurologist: A medical specialist in the treatment of nervous diseases.

Pharmacist: One who prepares and dispenses drugs and has a knowledge concerning their properties.

Psychiatrist: A medical doctor who specializes in the diseases of the mind. Professional responsibility includes appropriate drug disbursement.

AGENCY DIRECTORY

Information about a particular handicapping condition is often times not generally available. Parents, educators, health professionals, and everyone else who works with a particular identifiable handicap needs additional information about the handicap, services that are necessary and available, and the location of specified services. National organizations on specific disabilities or conditions focuses on information and support. Parent training and parent support groups offer general information, assistance, and support. Government agencies give information relating to laws and services. When help is needed there are many sources available to the handicapped person. When educational practices and general information appear sketchy and vague, help may be found through knowledgeable centers. These centers may be able to clarify the opportunities available to the handicapped person and a clearer route for the person directly involved with that individual who is handicapped.

Agency listings are given with addresses and telephone numbers when possible. Telephone numbers can, however, be obtained by dialing information in the city where the location is found. Do not give up if addresses are incorrect. Interagency information is available at any government center or clearing house. They are generally courteous and will assist the person when a need has been voiced to them.

The list of agencies used is largely found in a fact sheet distributed by NICHCY—The National Information Center for Children and Youth with Disabilities, P.O. Box 1492, Washington, D.C. 20013.

GOVERNMENT AGENCIES
Interprofessional Information

Administration for Children, Youth and Families
P.O. Box 1182
Washington, D.C. 20013
(202) 245-0347

Administration on Developmental Disabilities (DHHS)
329 D Humphrey Building
200 Independence Ave., S.W.
Washington, D.C. 20201
(202) 245-2890

Bureau of Maternal and Child Health
and Resources Development
Parklawn Building
5600 Fishers Lane
Rockville, MD 20857
(301) 443-2170

District Internal Revenue
Service - Tax Information
(800) 424-1040
(800) 424-FORM

National Institute of Neurological &
Communicative Disorders
NIH, Bldg. 31, Room 8A-06
Bethesda, MD 20892
(301) 496-4000

National Library Service for the Blind
and Physically Handicapped
Library of Congress
1291 Taylor Street, N.W.
Washington, D.C. 20542
(800) 424-8567

Office of Disease Prevention
and Health Promotion
National Health Information Center
P.O. Box 1133
Washington, D.C.
20013-1133, (800) 336-4797

Department of Health and Human Services
(Medicare Information and
Second Surgical Opinion Program)
Health Care Financing Administration
Baltimore, MD 21235

National Center for Education
in Maternal and Child Health
38th and R Streets, N.W.
Washington, D.C. 20625-8400

National Information Center for
Children & Youth with Handicaps (NICHCY)
P.O. Box 1492
Washington, D.C. 20013
(800) 999-5599
(703) 893-6061
(703) 893-8614 (TDD)

National Institute of Child
Health and Human Development
NIH, 9000 Rockville Pike
Bldg. 31, Room 2A03
Bethesda, MD 20892
(301) 496-3454

President's Committee on Employment
of People with Disabilities
1111 20th St., N.W., Suite 636
Washington, D.C. 20036-3470
(202) 653-5044
(202) 653-5050 (TDD)

Public Information Office
National Library of Medicine
Bethesda, MD 20894
(301) 496-4000

Senate Subcommittee on
Disability Policy
113 Hart Senate Office Bldg.
Washington, D.C. 20510
(202) 224-6265

Social Security Administration Hotline
(800) 234-5SSA
(800) 324-0778 (TDD)
(800) 392-0812 (in Mo./TDD)

Office of Special Education
and Rehabilitation Services
Clearinghouse on Disability Information
U.S. Dept. of Education
Room 3132, Switzer Bldg.,
330 C St., S.W.
Washington, D.C. 20202-2524
(202) 732-1723, (202) 732-1245

Volunteers in Service to America
Foster Grandparent Program
ACTION
Public Affairs Division
1100 Vermont Ave., N.W.
Washington, D.C. 20525

GENERAL INFORMATION

Public Agencies

STATE EDUCATION DEPARTMENT

The State Department staff can answer questions about special education and related services in your state. Many states have special manuals explaining the steps to take. Check to see if one is available. State Department officials are responsible for special education and related services programs in their state for preschool, elementary, and secondary age children.

STATE VOCATIONAL REHABILITATION AGENCY

The state vocational rehabilitation agency provides medical, therapeutics, counseling, education, training, and other services needed to prepare people with disabilities for work. This state agency will provide you with the address of the nearest rehabilitation office where you can discuss issues of eligibility and services with a counselor. The state vocational rehabilitation agency can also refer you to an independent living program in your state. Independent living programs provide services which enable adults with disabilities to live productively as members of their communities. The services might include, but are not limited to, information and referral, peer counseling, workshops, attendant care, and technical assistance.

OFFICE OF STATE COORDINATOR OF VOCATIONAL EDUCATION FOR HANDICAPPED STUDENTS

States receiving federal funds used for vocational education must assure that funding is used in programs which include students with handicaps. This office can tell you how your state funds are being used and provide you with information on current programs.

STATE MENTAL RETARDATION/DEVELOPMENTAL DISABILITIES AGENCIES

The functions of state mental retardation/developmental disabilities agencies vary from state to state. The general purpose of this office is to plan, administer and develop standards for state/local mental retardation/developmental disabilities programs provided in state-operated facilities and community-based programs. This office provides information about available services to families, consumers, educators and professionals.

STATE DEVELOPMENTAL DISABILITIES COUNCIL

Assisted by the U.S. Department of Health and Human Services' Administration on Developmental Disabilities, state councils plan and advocate for improvement in services for people with developmental disabilities. In addition, funding is made available for time-limited demonstration and stimulatory grant projects.

STATE MENTAL HEALTH AGENCIES

The functions of state mental health agencies vary from state to state. The general purposes of these offices are to plan, administer, and develop standards for state and local mental health programs such as state hospitals and community health centers. They can provide information to the consumer about mental illness and a resource list of contacts where you can go for help.

PROTECTION AND ADVOCACY AGENCY AND CLIENT ASSISTANCE PROGRAM

Protection and advocacy systems are responsible for pursuing legal, administrative and other remedies to protect the rights of people who are developmentally disabled or mentally ill, regardless of their age. Protection and advocacy agencies may provide information about health, residential, and social service in your are. Legal assistance is also available.

The Client Assistance Program provides assistance to individuals seeking and receiving vocational rehabilitation services. These services, provided under the Rehabilitation Act of 1973, include assisting in the pursuit of legal, administrative, and other appropriate remedies to ensure the protection of the rights of individuals with developmental disabilities.

PROGRAMS FOR CHILDREN WITH SPECIAL HEALTH CARE NEEDS

The U.S. Department of Health and Human Services' Office of Maternal and Child Health and Resource Development provides grants to states for direct medical and related services to children with handicapping conditions. Although services will vary from state to state, additional programs may be funded for retraining, research, special projects, genetic disease testing, and counseling services. For additional information about current grants and programs in your state, contact:

National Center for Education in Maternal and Child Health
38th and R Streets, NW
Washington, D.C. 20057.

UNIVERSITY AFFILIATED PROGRAMS

A national network of programs affiliated with universities and teaching hospitals, UAPs provides interdisciplinary training for professionals and paraprofessionals and offers programs and services for children with disabilities and their families. Some UAPs provide direct services for children and families. Individual UAPs have staff with expertise in a variety of areas and can provide information, technical assistance, and inservice training to agencies, service providers, parent groups, and others.

A listing of all University Affiliated Programs may be obtained by contacting:

The Maternal and Child Health Clearing House
38th and R Streets, N.W.
Washington, D.C. 20057.

DISABILITY AGENCIES

ATTENTION DEFICIT DISORDERS

**Children with Attention Deficit
 Disorders (C.H.A.D.D.)**
1859 N. Pine Island Road, Ste. 185
Plantation, FL 33322

MENTAL ILLNESS

**Federation of Families for Children's
 Mental Health**
National Mental Health Association
1021 Prince Street
Alexandria, VA 22314-2971

LEGAL RESPONSIBILITIES

Special education has been shaped by public law statues which employ a coherent approach for insuring educational opportunities to handicapped children. The following laws are presented in abbreviated form to summarize the procedures and safeguards enacted to shape and secure a "free and appropriate education for the handicapped."

They include the following:

1. Section 504 of the Rehabilitation Act of 1973.
2. P.L. 94-142 Education of the Handicapped Act of 1975.
3. P.L. 99-372 Handicapped Children's Protection Act of 1986.
4. P.L. 99-457 Education of the Handicapped Amendments of 1986.

P.L. 99-372 of 1986
Handicapped Children's Protection Act

This public law authorizes courts to award to parents of children with handicaps lawyer's fees who prevail in actions brought under P.L. 94-142.

REHABILITATION ACT of 1973
P.L. 93-112 (Section 504)

Purpose
"No otherwise qualified handicapped individual in the United States . . . shall, solely, by reason of . . . handicap, be excluded from participation in, be denied the benefit of, or be subjected to discrimination under any program or activity receiving federal financial assistance."

Population
Individuals included are those with handicaps involving physical or mental impairment that impairs or restrict one or more major life activities. Qualifying characteristics are inclusive of all handicaps found under P.L. 94-142. Alcoholism and drug addiction were added as handicapping conditions in 1977.

Components of the Law
Program Accessibility
No qualified handicapped person shall be excluded from participation in, be denied the benefit of, or otherwise be subjected to, discrimination under any program or activity because a recipient's facilities are inaccessible or unusable.

Preschool Elementary, and Secondary Adult Education
Educational programming that involves the above population shall receive or benefit from federal financial assistance to operate a designated program. Qualifying persons are those found in the Education of the Handicapped Act (P.L. 94-142).

Postsecondary Education
Qualifying programs and activities include postsecondary vocational educational training that benefit or receive federal financial assistance and to recipients that operate such programs. Individuals qualifying for such programs must meet academic and technical standards requisite for admission or participation.

Health, Welfare, and Social Services
Vocational programs may be limited to certain classes of individuals with handicaps with respect to health, welfare, and social services. Qualified handicapped persons who meet eligibility requirements are beneficiaries of the service.

Employment Practices
No qualified handicapped person shall be subjected to discrimination in employment under any program or activity which receives federal financial assistance. A qualified employable person, with reasonable accommodation, can perform the functions essential to job performance.

Amendment P.L. 99-506
"Supported employment begins when the labor of an individual with a disability is marketed to any employer, and service to the worker and/or employer is not time-limited but continuous throughout the

working life of that person or as long as necessary."

The Federal Aid Agency defines competitive work practice as work performed on a full or part-time basis, averaging at least 20 hours per week for each pay period and for which they employee is compensated. Funded supported employments are available through non-profit organizations, foundations, grants, local businesses, and community support as well as through government (state and federal) funding. Models, techniques, and strategies of various types are available. The Department of Vocational Rehabilitation is available to service the handicapped by providing information and services.

P.L. 99-457 EDUCATION of the HANDICAPPED AMENDMENTS of 1986

Purpose

"The Congress finds that there is an urgent and substantial need:
1. to enhance the development of handicapped infants and toddlers and to minimize their potential for developmental delay;
2. to reduce the educational costs to our society, including our nation's schools, by minimizing the need for special education and related services after (they) reach school age;
3. to minimize the likelihood of institutionalization of handicapped individuals and maximize the potential for their independent living in society; and
4. to enhance the capacity of families to meet the special needs of their infants and toddlers with handicaps."

Population

The two major groups involved in this mandate are the preschool grant program for three, four, and five year old handicapped children, and the infants and toddlers that are handicapped and at risk.

Components of the Law (3-5 year olds)

The law mandates and provides many incentives to serve the 3-5 age group for the right to educate. The population served does not have to be by diagnostic category so that labeling of a given child according to a specific category such as blind, learning disabled, etc. had been removed. Parental instruction is an allowable cost. Variations in the length of day or service model have been encouraged. School districts are encouraged to contact appropriate existing non-public school community preschool programs which provide a range of services and service models.

Handicapped Infants and Toddlers Program

The creation of Handicapped Infants and Toddlers Program was created for handicapped and at risk children from birth to three years and their families. "Early intervention" includes children who are experiencing developmental delays (cognitive, physical, language and speech, psychosocial, or self-help skills); physical or mental conditions which have a high probability for a delay (Downs Syndrome); "at risk" medically or environmentally if intervention is not included in their program. An interagency Coordinating Council was established to facilitate interagency dialogue.

Conclusion

The importance of interagency collaboration which maximizes the use of existing resources for handicapped children and their families is the major emphasis in this law. The established "Head Start" program is a primary resource for increased services of this population.

EDUCATION of the HANDICAPPED ACT of 1975 P.L. 94-142

Purpose

"(a) To insure that all handicapped children have available to them a free appropriate public education which includes special education and related services to meet their unique needs.
(b) To insure that the rights of handicapped children and their parents are protected.
(c) To assist states and localities to provide for the education of all handicapped children, and
(d) To assess and insure the effectiveness of efforts to educate those children.

Population

"Handicapped children" means those children evaluated as being mentally retarded, hard of hearing, deaf, speech impaired, visually handicapped, seriously emotionally disturbed, orthopedically handicapped, other health impaired, deaf-blind, multi-handicapped, or having specific learning disabilities, who, because of those impairments, need special education and related services. Testing and evaluation materials and procedures used for the purpose of evaluation and placement of handicapped children must be selected and administered so as not to be racially or culturally discriminatory."

Components of the Law

This law is very explicit and detailed with guidelines for school administration, trained personnel, resource centers and related services, and parents as well as the handicapped population itself. Certain components from this law have been selected for this book. For a complete and detailed outline of the law and its guidelines relating to the handicapping defined, you should request a copy from your State Department of Education.

General Provisions Component

In the Office of Special Education and Rehabilitative Services in the Department of Education is an Office of Special Education Programs which shall administer and carry out the provisions of this act. A Deputy Assistant Secretary shall head and be responsible for administering services. Assistance includes employment of handicapped individuals, removal of architectural barriers, enforcement of 30 day regulation policies, and determination of eligibility for financial assistance of programming for the handicapped.

Assistance for Education of All Handicapped Children Component

The State Office of Special Education programs has the policy that assumes all handicapped children have a right to a free appropriate public education from ages 3-21 (Sept. 1980-revised ages). Local educational agencies will maintain individual education programs. The state will establish safeguards and procedures of listing and evaluating materials for administration. In 1983 additional safeguards were enacted so that handicapped children shall receive assistance in private school settings. Procedural safeguards include the creation of a due process hearing system made available for the handicapped when disputes between parents and educators arise.

Center/Services to Meet Special Need of Handicapped Component

Regional resource and federal centers, services for deaf-blind children, early education for the handicapped children, programs for severely handicapped children, postsecondary education, secondary education and transitional services for handicapped youth are targeted in this component. They are as follows:

A. Regional resource center provides consultation, technical assistance, and training to State Educational Agency.

B. Deaf-blind children and youth provisions include special education and related services and vocational and transitional services. When age 21 is reached, program and services to facilitate their transition will be assured. Program components include diagnosis and educational evaluation; programs of adjustment, education and orientation; consultative counseling and training services.

C. Early education for handicapped services have been extended under P.L. 99-457 which is detailed in this chapter.

D. Programs for severely handicapped children services have been extended under P.L. 99-457 which is detailed in this chapter.

E. Postsecondary and transitional services have been extended under P.L. 99-506 which is detailed.

Training Personnel for the Education of the Handicapped Component

A. Clearinghouses
The law provides for a national clearinghouse on education of the handicapped to disseminate information and provide technical assistance on a national basis to parents, professionals, and other interested parties concerning programs relating to the handicapped and participation.

B. A national clearinghouse on Postsecondary Education for the purpose of providing information on available services and programs in postsecondary education. Both technical assistance and higher education opportunities is included with general information concerning scholarships, stipends, and allowances.

Higher Education and Adult Training for People with Handicaps (HEATH)
One DuPont Circle, N.W., Suite 800
Washington, D.C. 20036-1193

National Clearinghouse for Professions in Special Education
2021 K Street, N.W., Suite 315
Washington, D.C. 20006

National Information Center for Handicapped Children and Youth
P.O. Box 1492
Washington, D.C. 20013

Instructional Media for Handicapped Component

Special emphasis is placed on providing services for deaf educations through the establishment of a clearinghouse. The function of the clearinghouse is to establish a loan service of captioned films and educational media for deaf individuals, their parents, and other interested persons involved with the deaf.

National Information Center on Deafness (NICD)
800 Florida Avenue, N.E.
Washington, D.C. 20002

**Technology, Educational Media, and
Materials for the Handicapped Component**

The purpose of this component is advancing the use of new technology, media, and materials in education of handicapped students and the provision of early intervention to handicapped infants and toddlers. The specific purposes include determining, designing and adapting, assisting in, and dissemination of information concerning technology, educational media, and materials.

FEDERAL GOVERNMENT
DEPARTMENT OF EDUCATION
Office for Civil Rights
Regional Civil Rights Offices

REGION I

Connecticut, Maine, Massachusetts, New Hampshire, Rhode Island, Vermont

Regional Civil Rights Director
Office for Civil Rights, Region I
U.S. Department of Education, Room 222
John W. McCormack Post Office and Crthse Bldg.
Boston, MA 02109-4557

REGION II

New Jersey, New York, Puerto Rico, Virgin Islands

Regional Civil Rights Director
Office for Civil Rights, Region II
U.S. Department of Education
26 Federal Plaza, Room 33-130
New York, NY 10278-0082

REGION III

Delaware, District of Columbia, Maryland, Pennsylvania, Virginia, West Virginia

Regional Civil Rights Director
Office for Civil Rights, Region III
U.S. Department of Education
3535 Market Street, Room 6300
P.O. Box 13716
Philadelphia, PA 19104-3326

REGION IV

Alabama, Florida, Georgia, Kentucky, Mississippi, North Carolina, South Carolina, Tennessee

Regional Civil Rights Director
Office for Civil Rights, Region IV
U.S. Department of Education
101 Marietta St. Tower, Suite 2702
P.O. Box 1705
Atlanta, GA 30301-1705

REGION IX

Arizona, California, Hawaii, Nevada, Guam, Trust Territory of the Pacific Islands, American Samoa

Regional Civil Rights Director
Office for Civil Rights, Region IX
U.S. Department of Education
221 Main St., Suite 1020
San Francisco, CA 94105-1925
(415) 227-8040 TTY (415) 227-8124

REGION X

Alaska, Idaho, Oregon, Washington

Regional Civil Rights Director
Office for Civil Rights, Region X
U.S. Department of Education
915 Second Avenue, Room 3310
Seattle, WA 98174-1099
(206) 442-1636 TTY (206) 442-4542

NATIONAL RESOURCES

CLEARINGHOUSES

**Center for Special Education Technology
Council for Exceptional Children (CEC)**
1920 Association Drive
Reston, VA 22091-1589

**ERIC Clearinghouse on Handicapped and
Gifted Children**
Council for Exceptional Children (CEC)
1920 Association Drive
Reston, VA 229091-1589

**Higher Education and Adult Training for
People with Handicaps (HEATH)**
One Dupont Circle, N.W., Suite 800
Washington, D.C. 20036-1193

**National Clearinghouse for Professions
in Special Education**
2021 K Street, N.W., Suite 315
Washington, D.C. 20006

National Health Information Center
P.O. Box 1133
Washington, D.C. 20013-1133

**National Information Center
on Deafness
(NICD)**
800 Florida Avenue, N.E.
Washington, D.C. 20002

**National Rehabilitation Information
Center (NARIC)**
8455 Colesville Road, Suite 935
Silver Spring, MD 20910-3319

INFORMATION/ADVOCACY AGENCIES
FOR PARENTS

GENERAL INFORMATION

**American Bar Association
Center for Children and the Law**
1800 M Street, N.W., Suite 200
Washington, D.C. 20036
(202) 331-2250

Association for Retarded Citizens of the U.S.
2501 Avenue J
P.O. Box 6109
Arlington, Texas 76005
(817) 640-0204

**Association for the Care of
Children's Health**
3615 Wisconsin Ave., N.W.
Washington, D.C. 20016
(202) 244-1807

**Congress of Organizations of the
Physically Handicapped**
166630 Beverly Avenue
Tinley Park, IL 60477-1904
(708) 532-3566

Council for Exceptional Children
1920 Association Drive
Reston, VA 22019
(703) 620-3660

Council on Family Health
225 Park Ave., South, 17th Fl.
New York, NY 10003
(212) 598-3617

Deafpride, Inc.
1350 Potomac Avenue, S.E.
Washington, D.C. 20003

**ERIC Clearinghouse on
Handicapped and Gifted Children**
1929 Association Drive
Reston, VA 22091
(703) 620-3660

Lethbridge Society for Rare Disorders
100-542-7 Street, South Lethbridge
Alberta, Canada T1J 2H1
(403) 329-0665

Life Services for the Handicapped, Inc.
25 East 21st Street
New York, NY 10010
(212) 420-1500

Mental Health Law Project
2021 L Street, N.W.
8th Floor, Suite 800
Washington, D.C. 20036

**National Association for
Minorities with Disabilities**
3508 West North Avenue
Milwaukee, WI 53208
(414) 442-0522

**National Association of
Protection and Advocacy Systems**
900 2nd Street, N.E.
Suite 211
Washington, D.C. 20002
(202) 408-9514

**National Center for Youth
with Disabilities**
Adolescent Health Program
Univ. of Minnesota
Box 721-UMHC
Harvard Street at East River Road
Minneapolis, MN 55455
(800) 333-NCYD
(612) 626-2825

**National Digestive Diseases
Information Clearinghouse**
Box NDDIC
Bethesda, MD 20892
(301) 468-6344

National Disability Action Center
2021 L Street, N.W., Suite 800
Washington, D.C. 20036
(202) 467-5730 (Voice/TDD)

National Easter Seal Society
70 East Lake Street
Chicago, IL 60601
(800) 221-6827
(312) 726-6200
(312) 726-4258 (TDD)

**National Information Center for Children
and Youth with Handicaps (NICHCY)**
P.O. Box 1492
Washington, D.C. 20013
(800) 999-5599
(703) 893-6061

**National Information Center
for Educational Media**
4320 Mesa Granda, S.E.
Albuquerque, NM 87100

Legislators and the courts acknowledge the need for a unique education for the handicapped person. They recognized and established a policy that educational assistance must be centered around the disabled person's abilities rather than his disabilities. They gave it the label "special education." Public Law 94-142 requires that qualification for federal assistance includes:

Procedures to assure that, to the maximum extent appropriate, handicapped children, including children in public or private institutions or other care facilities, are educated with children who are not handicapped, and that special classes, separate schooling, or other removal of handicapped children from the regular educational environment occurs only when the nature or severity of the handicapped is such that education in regular classes with the use of supplementary aids and services cannot be achieved satisfactorily . . . .

Issues regarding the way handicapped children/ young adults were evaluated and placed in educational settings promoted this legislative proclamation with a prescribed method of procedure to be followed before federal educational funding would be released. The following considerations are addressed: the handicapped child's evaluation procedures; placement in "appropriate educational setting;" individual educational programs; and due process. Parental involve-ment and input into the whole educational process became a must by law.

EDUCATIONAL ASSESSMENT

A full evaluation of the child's educational needs must be assessed before placement in any special education program. This assessment must be completed before 30 school days have passed after an initial referral has been made. The purpose of the assessment is to determine all required information to validate a handicapping condition and identify the specific condition; show need for special education and related services; and conduct instructional planning.

EDUCATIONAL DECISION MAKING DOMAINS

The following domains have been established for assessment analysis. Formal and informal assessment is made from selected domain areas. These areas include the following:

Physical functioning:
- Receptive processes including vision, hearing, haptic/tactile and kinesthetic functioning.
- Expressive processes including speech mechanism, motor/psychomotor skills, and medical/health conditions.

Mental Integration Functioning:
- Mental subnormal functioning (intelligence level).
- Thinking processes and skills.

Communication Functioning:
- Language, both verbal and nonverbal communication, modes of communication, voice, fluency.

Educational Functioning:
- Content areas of achievement (reading skills, comprehensive, basic reading skills, mathematics-written expression-listening-learning styles).

Environmental Influences:
- Family history–impact of home, school, and community, dominant language, family relationships, educational history, cultural/economic factors, student involvement with his whole environment.

Vocational Functioning:
- work behavior
- job skills/preferences
- abilities
- special needs

Social competence:
- adaptive behaviors (personal/daily, community, communication skills and independent living and social responsibility) to meet environmental demands.

Recreational competence:
- Functioning in terms of free time and personal social involvement

A written assessment is made and upon this assessment an education placement will be planned by a selected group of professionals qualified to discuss with the parents a program for the handicapped child/youth in his/her "least restrictive environment." This is referred to the ARC committee (ARC).

PLACEMENT IN APPROPRIATE EDUCATIONAL SETTING "LEAST RESTRICTIVE ENVIRONMENT"

"Least restrictive environment" means the educational setting in which the identified child or youth can effectively function and perform yet also interact with non-handicapped age peers. Removal from the regular classroom occurs when the nature and severity of the handicapping condition forces alternate or modified educational programming. Modifications, supplementary services, and supplementary aids are influencing factors that regulate "least restrictive environment" alternatives.

Modifications: Physical environment change; use of supplementary aids and services; reorganizing staff patterns; use of alternative learning style, adapter curricula or training personnel is special techniques in behavior and instruction.

Supplementary services: includes school nurse, physical therapist, occupational therapist, psychologist, school counselor, language interpreter.

Supplementary aids: includes language print books, braille writers, communication boards, classroom aids, tape recorders, etc.

Program placement alternative settings could be selected from the regular school, special day school, residential facility, residential school, community, hospital, and home.

Time allotted in these various alternative settings is decided and transportation options are made known at this time. The Admissions and Release Committee (ARC) makes the decision as to the "least restrictive environment" for the individual and initiates an individual educational plan.

INDIVIDUAL EDUCATIONAL PROGRAM (IEP)

An "IEP" is an Individual Educational Program developed by an Admission and Release Committee (ARC) to meet the special educational needs of a handicapped child with a specific educational handicap. This written plan contains the required components that implement the instructional planning.

The IEP serves different purposes. It is a management document for special education programming and the related services required. The individual's current functioning level and expected learning is communicated through the IEP. It monitors a child's progress as well as evaluates the student's progress toward meeting projected outcomes. It focuses on and tries to resolve differences between parents and the school.

Individual Educational Programs (IEPs) must include the following components:

Present levels of performance:
A written document of the educational/behavioral assessment data which includes the individuals strength and weaknesses in academic and non-academic areas. It reflects health, social, and vocational competencies. The impact of the educational performance is stated in each educational domain area. No categorical label can substitute for levels of performance. If test scores are included they must be stated and explained.

Annual Goals:
The annual goals are related to an area of need which requires special intervention. Annual goals are identified and written in the level of performance document. They focus on an instructional area naming a particular skill needed to perform successfully in that subject or instructional area.

Short Term Memory:
Short term objectives are concise, measurable statements which serve as guide for instructional planning. They are written in such a way that the disabled individual's behavior is stated. These objectives are stated in such a way so that they follow instructional sequencing. Each annual goal found in the IEP must have subskill objectives. It becomes a formal part of the IEP.

A short term goal contains the following components:
1. A statement of the behavior that is to be performed.
2. The condition under which the behavior is to be performed (where-when-how-etc.).

3. The level of performance–how rapid, percentage or proportion of current responses.

Specially Designated Instruction and Related Services:

"Specially designed instruction" includes physical and environmental adaptations which are not ordinary features found in a regular class setting. Instructional content, methods, materials, techniques, and media are included in this section of the Individual Educational Program.

Adaptation and modification are key issues in involving a specially designed program. They must be necessary for fulfilling either an annual goal or short term objective(s).

Support and related services are needed to benefit from special education services. This must be corrective or developmental by nature. They must not be solely for medical, health, or aesthetic reasons.

Participation In Regular Education Program:

Time spent with children and youth in a regular educational program was a major concern of legislation in planning P.L. 94-142. Each I.E.P. is required to document time spent, the level of the class, and in what area of the regular educational program they will be placed.

Both academic and nonacademic areas/activities are identified and used. Modifications and adaptations are written into the program (the beginning and ending dates, when participation will occur, and who is responsible for this participation.

Educational programs and services available for the handicapped child include art, music, industrial arts, consumer and homemaking education, and vocational education. Physical education services include children in separate facilities, participation in regular physical education programs, and designed adaptive physical education if prescribed in the child's Individual Educational Program (IEP).

EVALUATION OF INDIVIDUAL EDUCATIONAL PROGRAM

Periodical checks of mastery of short term instructional objectives are required. Achievement of the goals is dependent on whether IEP programming needs to be changed. Each person who is assigned to a particular object is responsible for evaluating the procedure. Parent involvement is required when revisions are necessary.

Annual goals are also periodically checked. An I.E.P. meeting is often scheduled at the end of the year for evaluation and further planning for the disabled student. Changes in an Individual Educational Plan require parents' or guardians' signatures when possible. Members of the Admissions and Releases Committee

(ARC) are to be a part of each scheduled meeting.

When an annual or short term goal has not been met, further attention is given. Suggestions such as to level placement, the educational objective itself, inter-professional involvement to accomplish the goal may cause revision and change of a given goal. A given objective may not be able to be accomplished at a particular time or within a particular scheduled time period.

DUE PROCESS HEARINGS

When parents or school educators are unable to come to an agreement about special education eligibility, appropriate programming, and placement, they may seek outside arbitration. The procedural safeguard is called a "due process hearing."

Parent participation is required when a disabled child or youth qualifies for special education. They are as follows:

1. Written notice to parents must be given before the school initiates a change or refuses to initiate a change;
2. I.E.P. participation is a direct responsibility of the parent;
3. Formal evaluation and assessments as well as initial placement require written, informed parental consent; educational records held by the school may be inspected and reviewed by parents.

Due Process Hearing Systems vary from state to state. State Educational Agencies (SEA) may conduct a hearing. Their decision may be appealed to a state or federal court. Local school districts (or other public agency educating the child) may conduct a hearing. The decision may be appealed to the SEA for state level review, and a final review may be taken to the state or federal courts if decisions rendered are not functional for the handicapped person. Voluntary mediation is used in some states where a third party decides the disagreement between the parent and school sector.

A due process hearing may be requested by parents when the following conditions have failed to be met:

1. School system proposes to initiate or change identification, evaluation, or educational placement;
2. School system proposes to initiate or change the provisions of free appropriate public education to a child;
3. School system fails to initiate or change in identification, evaluation, or educational placement;
4. School system fails to initiate or change the provision of free appropriate public education to a child;
5. The parent requests and the school district

refuses or fails to amend the educational records of a child.

Hearing officers are arbitrators in disputes between school systems and parents. Each school district or public agency which conducts due process hearings maintains a list of persons who serve as hearing officers with their qualifications. Direct involvement in the educational system is essential in becoming a hearing officer. The hearing officer cannot have a personal or professional interest which would make him or her favor a particular side. No employee involved in the education or care of the child can be used.

Pre-hearing procedures provide information for both sides to present their position at the hearing. Pre-hearing conferences include:

1. The specific legal and factual issues to be addressed;
2. Witnesses to be used and documentaries that will be produced at the hearing;
3. Each party has the right to present evidence and cross-examine witnesses;
4. A written or electronic word-for-word transcript of the hearing must be prepared and made available to both parties.

The burden of proof is placed on the party requesting the hearing. If, however, the issue involves placement outside the regular educational environment, the burden of proof is on the school. Hearing officers may grant extensions of time for conducting and completing a hearing.

A hearing decision is a written document issued to both parties no later than 45 days after the request for hearing has been received by the educational system or agency involved. The hearing decision is considered final unless appealed to the State Education Association (SEA) within the time period set by state administration procedures. The SEA may do an impartial review if the dissatisfied party requests it. A state or federal court becomes involved when a decision is challenged. Suits can be brought to either setting but not both. The Handicapped Child's Protection Act of 1986 (P.L. 99-372) allows the award of fees and other costs to parents who win due process hearing or court cases.

The special education program is complicated by legal interpretation and often times fails because of procedural mismanagement. When a child qualifies for assistance these safeguards might be considered so that a free and appropriate education is productive to the individual involved:

- class size—consider numbers in the class
- class arrangement—consider age, grade, and disability
- pupil-teacher ratio—can IEP be implemented?
- classroom atmosphere—consider whether rapport can be established and proper control maintained
- curriculum offerings
- related services—how much and how often?
- methods and materials—are their specified variations available to meet your child's needs?
- type of problem—is appropriate setting available with trained personnel?
- amount of time—is specific disability addressed effectively considered?
- grading system—will educational changes affect terminal degree?
- evaluation procedures—who will evaluate the IEP program?

CONCLUSION

This book has been designed to assist those persons who desire basic information and ideas concerning handicapping. After teaching the introductory exceptional child course for the past twenty years, this author still finds it difficult to assume what is basic. The involvement of so many professions continues to complicate the problem.

Each chapter, purposefully, lists professional organizations, agencies and educational interest groups pertaining to its particular topic. The book is an attempt to aid you in your search for help and understanding. Since opinions vary and, at times, conflict, you must continue your search for updated findings.

Agencies are formed centering and focusing on a particular interest group. It was impossible to list each agency. Omission of a particular agency does not mean it lacks authenticity, or agencies listed may not be the best for your particular interest. You may need to search for further assistance through different agencies. In my opinion, I have never found a more conscientious and sensitive group of people than those involved in an agency interest.

In closing, I can only wish you good luck and may God bless you with the pearls that he has entrusted to your care and keeping.

NOTES

NOTES

BY THE SAME AUTHOR

Reading, Writing: A Tutorial Guide in the Language Arts – 2nd Edition
by
Earl S. Zehr

This handbook contains step-by-step writing lessons for tutors who are assisting upper elementary and secondary age students in improving their reading skills through writing. Special emphasis is placed on building a better self-image for "re-entry" into educational programing.

Includes a language arts continuum.

Rowan Mountain Press

0-926487-08-6 • $12.00

vi + 86 p.